THE SOUL
AND HANDWRITING

Scriptor Books

Ania Teillard

THE SOUL
AND HANDWRITING

Translated by
Edward O'Neill

Edited by
Lorraine Herbert and Kathryn Goulandris

Scriptor 🏛 *Books*

an imprint of
The British Academy of Graphology
London

First published in France
"L'Ame et l'Ecriture", by Ania Teillard
Publisher: Editions Traditionnelles

French Edition copyright © Editions Traditionnelles

English Edition first published in 1993 by
SCRIPTOR BOOKS, an imprint of
The British Academy of Graphology (Limited by guarantee)
in association with The London College of Graphology Ltd,
75 Quinta Drive, Barnet, Herts. EN5 3DA

Editorial Office: 123 Bickenhall Mansions,
London W1H 3LB

A CIP catalogue record for this book
is available from the British Library.

ISBN 0-9513700-5-7

Design and Production by

EuroBuro '92   Brigitte Froud
                 London, Tel 081-788 3289

CONTENTS

6

PART TWO

FOREWORD

Ania Teillard is a revered name in the graphological and psychoanalytical world in Europe. She was the first to research the link between depth psychology and graphology and to see Jung's psychological types through the handwriting.

Starting from the observation of the scriptural movement and its inherent symbolism, she explored the attitudes and their motivations. She devoted her life to this study, working closely with C.G. Jung for over 20 years and was greatly influenced by his brilliance and understanding of the human mind.

"The Soul and Handwriting" is one of the ten greatest books written on graphology. Therefore is seemed to me totally absurd that it had never been published in English.

It is almost 40 years since "L'Ame et l'Ecriture" first appeared in France and Germany. It has been translated into most European languages and has never stayed out of print for more than a couple of months. It was unfair that English-speaking people should be deprived of such a classic. So I decided that something had to be done. The enterprise started with a search for a translator. Naturally I stumbled on that most vulgar of obstacles: money. Then I remembered meeting Ed O'Neill from New York 10 years ago, who told me that he had translated "The Soul and Handwriting". "It was a labour of love" he said and offered me a copy. I couldn't believe my luck.

Edward O'Neill is one of those rare beings; somewhere between a sage and an angel; he is modest, unassuming, totally allocentric and good, with a gentle sense of humour and tremendous sensitivity. Now in his seventies, he is still studying, translating, learning and lecturing.

The next step was to ask the permission of the French publishers. To my astonishment the result was a polite but uncompromising "Non"! The late "patron" was not exactly an Anglophile. It took me almost 10 years of writing, telephoning, visiting and arguing before an agreement was finally reached.

In the meantime **Scriptor Books** has commissioned translations and published three other classic books (by Gabrielle Beauchataud, Emile Caille and J.-Ch.Gille-Maisani) and I thought that finally the great Teillard was now on its way. However, the biggest disappointment was yet to come: Funds! The text was translated, the permission granted and the publishing company founded, but still I could not proceed with the final product. It was most disappointing.

It seemed I would have to wait yet another year or two. But only a couple of months later another stroke of luck touched the book. **Nicholas Scott**, a man who shares my passion for the study of graphology came to see me one evening. The subject of publications came up and I explained the situation to him. As soon as he heard about our plight, he offered to sponsor not only the publication of "The Soul and Handwriting", but also the next book in line, Max Pulver's "The Symbolism of Handwriting", also translated by Ed O'Neill.

This is a most touching gesture which will be appreciated by thousands of people now and by generations of English-speaking graphologists to come. Ed O'Neill and Nicholas Scott have given us the chance to study and learn from two of the most exquisite and important books on graphology.

RENNA NEZOS

Founder and Principal of The British Academy of Graphology

PREFACE

*The title alone of Mme. Teillard's book, **The Soul and Handwriting**, which seems so simple, is symbolic and programmatic. It represents both the placing of graphology among the sciences, and a revolution in practice. First of all, take the word "Soul." What we most often find on the cover pages of works on handwriting is the word "Character." In the case of Crépieux-Jamin particularly, this word is understood in its current sense, as a collection of good or bad qualities which govern the conduct of human beings towards each other. The writer is good, bad, frank, cunning, egoistic, generous, choleric, calm, he inspires confidence or he doesn't, etc..... These are the words that, in our everyday life, we use about him. The Soul, on the other hand, taken by itself, apart from any particular mode of conduct, is the mysterious core of the person, the warm, dynamic centre of the psyche, the dwelling place of the fundamental sensibilities of the living being: his feelings, his memories (and those from the species' dim and distant past) his wishes and desires, even his thought processes.*

Again, the majority of titles of graphological works mention "Handwriting" first of all. "Handwriting and Character" is the generic title of this type of work. This word order symbolises a stage in graphology, one in which Handwriting is the object of study, the exciting novelty, where-as the subject of Character is ground that was covered a long time ago.

Where previously we had discovered its expressive value through intuitive flashes, handwriting was now examined in order to describe its anatomy, its physiology, to define all its aspects (the signs) and gradually compile a catalogue of the latters' correspondences with known character traits. The founder, Hippolyte Michon, raised graphology to its present

*level by a single stroke of genius, but he lacked a scientific
psychology, which has only recently been established. After
him, the work of painstaking description, classification and
methodology was undertaken in masterful fashion by
Crépieux-Jamin and completed by a number of foreign
researchers.*

*The work of patient observation, measurement and
statistical analysis is still in progress, but we can say that, even
though detailed discoveries will continue to be made
indefinitely, the most important laboratory work is finished
and its chief findings established.*

The Soul and Handwriting *- the title alone finally places
graphology in its true element: graphology is, indeed, an
applied branch of psychology: the latter, apart from its general
line of business, which deals with psychic content, has
diversified into several specialised branches, among which we
include* **Characterology,** *or the science of the laws of character
composition, which comprises typology (the description of the
several types in whom these laws are encapsulated) and
finally, the different* **sciences of expression** *amongst which
graphology takes its place.*

*These sciences of expression owe their existence to a law of
immense scope that seems to govern living (and perhaps even
inanimate Nature!) and implies an order of Nature, according
to whose law, every feeling (either conscious or unconscious
psychic content) should be manifested outwardly by an
expression.*

*All expressions, whether conscious or unconscious, seem
to constitute a universal language co-extensive with all life,
and immediately perceptible by means of* **symbols.** *Every
form, every movement, every gesture, even of vegetable life, is
significant of its being or of this or that quality of its being.
But, among man's manifestations, handwriting is the stratum
of the richest unconscious significance that we have found and
it is this discovery that has opened the way to graphology.*

Thus, general psychology, characterology, typology, and the science of expression, including graphology, belong together and progress at the same pace. This association is essential. It is, in fact, difficult for a specialist in expression to discover in the phenomena he is studying, the manifestation of psychic content of which he is ignorant. That is why Crépieux-Jamin, for example, writing before the advent of modern psychology in the wake of psychoanalysis and the progress of contemporary psychiatry, could find in handwriting only the "character traits" already known to classical psychology. With the exploration of the unconscious, the discovery of the complexes, with the works of Janet, Freud, Jung, Adler and their rivals, a multitude of new meanings can be uncovered in handwriting.

The book we are going to read is one remarkable offspring of this expansion of graphology. It uses Jaminian terminology and material, which are summarised at the end of the book in clear explanatory terms and in a dictionary, so that the reader on first meeting with this new approach to graphology, has traditional tools to work with, which, together with these appendices, constitutes a manual which is self-sufficient. But, Ania Teillard's interpretations no longer have anything in common with what was current before Klages and Pulver, to mention only those two masters.

What is special here is her use of analytical psychology: the correspondences between Jung's typology and graphology are her personal discovery. She strives to uncover, not the writer's empirical character, but its unconscious basis and inner structure.

What I admire in Ania Teillard's work is that it breaks with ordinary books on graphology, in which study of the writing holds first place: here, it is the study of the human soul and a passionate attention to psychology that guide the use of graphology, and stir up experiences, find correspondences. What is most lacking, indeed, in newly-fledged graphologists

14

is not the application - rather easy to acquire - of technique: it is, in addition to an inborn sensitivity to symbols, a knowledge of the human soul, and a burning desire to make progress in it. When we have these preconditions, we can rapidly advance in graphology. Conversely, the study of graphology by psychologists who are new to the subject, introduces them immediately and concretely to the living core of psychology and opens up to their minds an unexpected career of singular personal and social value. Ania Teillard has the burning desire of which I have just spoken, and her book has the merit of constantly holding open doors that enable the soul and the handwriting to communicate.

In addition, one can say that this work has foundations of a unique quality. Ania Teillard-Mendelssohn has studied with Jung and Klages, whose doctrines have had a decisive influence on her: she has worked with Pulver, and has been in correspondence with Saudek, Crépieux-Jamin, and everyone of importance in European graphology.

For many years she has combined her work as a psychoanalyst with graphology and it is precisely the union of these two spheres that constitute her main contribution to the psychological disciplines.

These are singularly brilliant claims upon the attention of the French public, who are turning to graphology in ever greater numbers.

No guide could be more interesting and more useful than the book I have the honour of introducing to people.

MAURICE DELAMAIN [*]

(*) *Translater's note* : Former President of the French Graphological Society, now regrettably deceased, as is Ania Teillard.

AUTHOR'S NOTE

It is with a deep joy that I am witness to the re-printing of this book, and I thank Traditional Publications for having shown enough confidence in this work to revive it.

*Those familiar with **The Soul and Handwriting** will find it unchanged. In fact, the concepts, un-edited since its first appearance, have given proof of their worth and have been included in the general teaching of graphology. The contribution of depth psychology to the study of handwriting has today been accepted without reservations.*

If I chose depth psychology as a basis for my graphological research, it is because it is the only one that embraces the unconscious as well as the conscious, thus exploring the totality of the psyche, sometimes including its very contradictions.

Modern psychology is above all, dynamic, sustained by the ever-renewed experiences of man.

Certainly, this book does not determine my position vis-a-vis new methods in graphology. I propose to approach them in another work. Here, it is only a question of briefly expounding my perspective of man and of offering a practical and tested work method.

The new edition of this book is a further testimony to the memory of Professor Jung. Moreover, I would like to link with it the names of Mr. Delamain, who has presented my work to French readers, and Mme. Beauchataud, who has helped me so much in producing it.

PART ONE

INTRODUCTION

Problems of Graphology and the Graphologist

Graphology is based on the long-held premise that *handwriting reflects the person*. There exist undeniably, relationships between the diverse graphic signs that form an individual's writing trail and the psychic make-up of the writer. These relationships are not based on a mathematical theory and cannot be established by scientific methods alone. We ought therefore to accept as a postulate what practice has made evident. The co-ordination of the graphic signs and their psychological interpretation, together with well thought-out syndromes, will result in a portrait which is true to the writer.

What is the link between the graphic sign and its psychological meaning? *That link is the symbol.* Apart from a few species of signs (pressure, tremors, breaks, ataxia), which are partly psychological, handwriting is essentially symbolic.

Max Pulver, in his book, *Die Symbolik der Handschrift*, makes this concept the cornerstone of his graphological system. Some individuals have a particular intuitive sense allowing them to feel the meaning inherent in the graphic forms. A good graphologist is one who re-lives the symbolic meaning of the signs or groups of signs and then combines them by means of his understanding of their significance. The more capable he is of marshalling the precisely formulated truths associated with the graphic signs, the richer and more accurate his portraits will be. The wider his experience, the better he will be able to understand a writing by analogy with others which are familiar to him.

Analytic methods are simply aids, technical expediencies or useful guidelines. It is the creative act that is of central importance. The graphologist makes use of his vocabulary of signs and the interpretations attached to them, much as a composer combines musical notes to compose a fugue or a minuet.

Graphology is comprised of two elements: *the graphic signs and their interpretation*.

The central problem of graphology is therefore that of the relationship between the *visible elements* (the signs of the writing) and the *invisible elements* (the psychological data).

The *visible elements* were named and classified in a fairly definitive way by Michon and Crépieux-Jamin. But as far as the *invisible psychological elements* are concerned, the question becomes more complex. The early masters found, as equivalents of graphic signs, character traits, virtues and faults, in accordance with the vocabulary of the time. They responded to the public's interest, therefore, without submitting this aspect of graphology to verification. These qualities of character, however: goodness, wickedness, frankness, dissimulation, are too broad, too charged with personal biases and prejudices of all kinds, to be made the subject of a scientific classification.

We would be on much surer ground if, instead of looking for fixed properties of character, we studied *reactions - the play of the functions, the play of the tendencies* - briefly, the soul's stirrings, *the human being's dynamism.* Later on, it will be shown that character traits are merely qualities derived from these fundamental tendencies. Today, therefore, it is a question of comparing the classification of signs by Michon and Crépieux-Jamin with the recent theories that psychology has placed at our disposal.

Certainly, the majority of the observations of these authors are correct and true today. Others, however, no longer correspond to our time. To cite one example: Crépieux-Jamin, in his *A B C de la Graphologie*, says of pale handwriting, that it is, "frequent in young girls whose faculties are asleep, not yet developed." The young girls of today are quite different from those of 1900. Their writing, far from being pale, is often more energetic and independent than that of boys.

The graphologist does not have to invent a new psychology. There are enough methods and typologies from which to choose the one best suited to his requirements.

As far as I am concerned, after much research, I have settled for *depth psychology* (Freud, Jung, Adler) and above all C.G.Jung's typology (the attitude types: Extraversion and Introversion, and the functional types: Thinking, Feeling, Sensation, Intuition), which seem the closest to life, the most flexible and the most manageable [1].

In any case, graphologists have always had recourse to typologies : from the ancient concepts of the four

---

(1) According to the usage adopted in France, I mean by the word "Psychoanalysis", Freud's Psychoanalysis, Adler's Individual Psychology and Jung's Analytical Psychology, while taking into account the difference between the three doctrines. The term "Depth Psychology" embraces all three equally. Jung, after his parting with Freud, gave his method the name of *Analytical Psychology.* Later on, he named it *Complex Psychology* : this term particularly applies to his doctrine of psychology as set out in his work.

temperaments (Bilious, Nervous, Sanguine, Lymphatic, used by Dr. Carton, and subsequently by Crépieux-Jamin) to the astrological types (Mars, Jupiter, Venus, Saturn, Mercury, Moon, Sun), right up to the classification of St. Morand, who divided individuals into three categories: the super-vital, the subvital and the balanced.

Klages rejects existing typologies and, relying mainly on the idea of an insurmountable antagonism between the soul and the mind, applies to handwriting the classifications that derive from that idea. Max Pulver, the most advanced of the graphologists, is opposed, on the other hand, to the introduction of esoteric ideas into the realm of graphology. He uses, as I do, the concept of depth psychology and of psychopathology (Kretschmer and others).

The great advantage of these concepts is that they are known throughout the world and the graphologist who relies on them is safe in the knowledge that he is not isolated, but that the terminology is common to all. He will find, in present-day psychology, living types who reflect not only the sick or neurotic but the healthy person as well. The neuroses are not rare abnormalities, but exaggerations of certain characteristics of normal people. Firmly established neuroses become part of the character.

Jung's typology agrees with Dr. Kretschmer's, which is based on *constitution* : the schizothyme (lean, bony, sensitive, cold, entrenched within himself, with a methodical and abstract mind) and the cyclothyme (roundish, jovial, social, productive, but subject to periods of melancholy). The schizothyme corresponds, broadly, to Jung's *introvert*, the cyclothyme to the *extravert*. The same correspondence exists between Dr. Corman's "contracted" and "released" subjects.

Every typology, as we all know, includes an arbitrary element. The correlation between the above-mentioned three, however, would seem to confirm their correctness as well as their usefulness.

It should be noted that classification of individuals into the attitude-types of *introversion* and *extraversion* makes no distinction as to the superiority or otherwise of these types.

Similarly the typology of the functions - *Thinking, Intuition, Feeling* and *Sensation* - which will be studied further on, are all equally necessary to the life of the individual and to the harmonious balance of society. The types springing from them can have equal moral and social worth.

Finally, to anticipate any objections, it should be pointed out that the concept of *type* does not exclude idiosyncrasies or originality. On the contrary, the most diversified traits and details of character may be found amongst people who have been classified as having the same attitude or the same dominant function.

As to the various graphological methods, one should not dwell too much on their differences. All systems derive from a single source : that of Michon and his predecessors. Around 1900, Klages, the undisputed leader of the German school, learnt of the essential concepts of French graphology from Hans Busse, who translated Crépieux-Jamin's work. In his book, *Handschrift und Charakter* [1], he brought to this new science his philosophical and physiognomical ideas, while retaining all Crépieux-Jamin's observations and classifications of signs. He rejected the idea of the "resultants," but adopted the Jaminian principle according to which it is the *initial overall impression* that decides the value of a handwriting. His only substitution was the concept of the *formniwo* in place of the French idea of *harmony* or *lack of harmony*. He remodelled the static ideal of harmony into a dynamic concept of "the life inherent in the writing," of "authenticity of life," which should not be confused with

---

(1) The French translation of this work is published by Niestlé et Delachâux under the title, *L'Expression du Caractère dans l'Ecriture*.

"Vitality", or "Vital impulse", or "Affectivity". It is quite clear that what we have here is, a new philosophical orientation and not a change of a graphological nature, as such.

Saudek, the Czech graphologist, in his books, *Experimentelle Graphologie* and *Wissenschaftliche Graphologie* always relied on the Jaminian method, which he enhanced by the very rejection of KIages's philosophical ideas.

Pulver, leader of the Swiss school, also recognised in *Die Symbolik der Handschrift* that the main point of departure for all scientific graphology started with the French school.

The distinction between the different schools lies in the psychological basis and not the graphological basis of their concepts. The nomenclature of the signs, their classification and meaning are the same for everyone except for a few nuances in interpretation.

This precept is essential in the interest of our science and its development. We must establish *a graphology that encompasses every method* and not create numbers of opposing schools that do not even understand one another. How can we hope to inspire confidence in the public, or create a teaching profession, if we do not start from the same basis?

A common basis does, however exist. There is proof of it in the fact that handwriting analyses performed by graphologists who are adherents of different systems, reach the same conclusions. A good graphologist of the French school will discern, just as effectively as a competent Swiss, American or German colleague, a writer's intellectual or moral worth.

The dictionary, at the back of this book, which groups several interpretations of the same signs given by different authors, demonstrates that in these evaluations only minimal differences exist, due to the fact of there being several observers.

The different schools should therefore, seek to enrich each other by their mutual contributions in order to build on the ground already acquired. Having clarified the pioneering role of the Jaminian school, it should, however, be appreciated that this has now been superseded from the standpoint of psychology, particularly with regard to the concept of *Resultants*.

All too frequently a graphologist, in an attempt to go further, prefers to build *his* system, *his* method, which will be totally different to all the previous ones, rather than relying on the works of his contemporaries.

Thus we come to the *psychological problem of the graphologist himself.*

Because graphology considers handwriting in its symbolic aspects, the graphologist's own personality assumes an essential importance, since it is he who must interpret these symbols. A handwriting will only be as clear as the mirror which reflects it.

The responsibility for recreating the inner impulse, as expressed by a sign, in order to transpose it into a psychological value, lies with the graphologist. In graphology, however, as in every psychology, the graphologist is both judge and defendant. The personal factor comes into play from the first moment of seeing a writing. One sees what one is best able to see. This personal evaluation assumes an even greater importance when it comes to the act of formulating and communicating what one has observed.

C.G.Jung, in the introduction of his book, *Psychological Types,* says in this connection: "In no field more than in psychology, is it necessary for the observer or the scientist to be equal to the task: in other words capable of seeing things from different angles. Awareness of the subjective factor in all knowledge, especially in psychological knowledge, is a prerequisite for unbiased and scientific understanding of a psyche, since that of the subject and observer may be quite different. This condition is only fulfilled if the observer is sufficiently *conscious of what he is*, if he has, to a large degree, freed himself from conditioning influences, collective judgements and opinions and consequently arrived at a clear conception of his own individuality".

Everyone knows how much the graphologist's psychological structure determines the portrait he paints. Dr. Allendy, in his excellent book, *L'Enfance Méconnue*, deprecates the tendency of some teachers and parents to project their own complexes onto children. Projections must be avoided in analyses at all costs.

To cite but one example, a graphologist who comes from a modest background, upon seeing a socialite's handwriting, might be tempted to be pitiless in telling this "parasite" some hard truths, or on the other hand, be over-impressed with the elegance of the writing. In either case, the excessive subjectivity of the graphologist will have let his own inferiority complex get the better of him.

Our first duty is *objectivity*. We should aspire to broaden our field of consciousness as much as possible and keep spotless the mirror in which we reflect the handwriting. This can only be done by virtue of a solid psychological education and a profound self-knowledge. Here, psychoanalysis can render great service. By its methods of exploring the unconscious and by allowing experiences to be lived through, it can enlighten a graphologist about his own problems and in seeing himself more clearly, allow him to judge others more objectively.

To sum up, we would say that the problems of graphology are inseparable from those of the graphologist, and that in both cases, the problems are of a psychological nature.

Today, therefore, it is no longer a matter of extending graphology, but of going in depth.

Depth Psychology

Before discussing graphological methods, it is important to introduce the reader to the psychology that serves as the basis of this work. The latter, though still suspect in the eyes of the psychological establishment and of some in the medical profession, has nevertheless interested recent observers in the fields of mental science, from moralists to philosophers, from practitioners of Wertheimer's *Gestalttheorie* to existentialists, behaviourists, behavioural psychologists, even to theologians. The theatre, the novel, the cinema, have all been greatly influenced by psychology. All those concerned with the human being have borrowed from this source and have drawn lessons from it.

If graphology does not profit from this evolution it could become isolated and its progress arrested.

To begin with character is described from the viewpoint of depth psychology, as a preliminary to the fuller explanation in the second part of this work, in which I will expand on the methods for discovering character through the medium of handwriting.

It is not my intention to explain elementary principles of graphology. Here it will be sufficient to include them in the dictionary at the end of the book.

The *Introductory Course in Graphology* performs this function for my readers.

THE STRUCTURE OF THE PSYCHE

Analytical psychology considers the *psyche* as an indivisible whole composed of more or less conscious contents, leading from an outer layer, in the full light of consciousness, to deeper layers that are completely unknown to ourselves.

The outer layer, the most easily accessible, is the *conscious* one. It is through this that we enter into a relationship with the world around us. It comprises all the outer aspects of our personality or *Persona* (from *personare* : to speak through. Persona refers to the mask worn by the actors of the ancient theatre). The Persona is shaped largely by the environment and education.

The underlying layer is the *personal* or individual unconscious : and the third, a deeper one, the *collective* or universal unconscious [1].

No clear dividing lines exist between these three layers. Each, however, has its particular mode of reaction and as a result of their constant fluctuations, all three penetrate and interact with each other.

---

(1) The term *unconscious* seems preferable to *subconscious*, which was used in the early days of psychoanalysis.

Only a small part of our life evolves in the clarity of consciousness. Our conscious life is nothing more than "a shellfish in the night scudding over the ocean of our unconscious" (Jung).

The States of Consciousness

We could consider the conscious as an organ permitting us to orientate ourselves in the outside world. Apart from the will, it embraces a large part of the affective tendencies and the elements commonly associated with an individual's character. The conscious is not in perpetual motion; it is subject to interruptions. The unconscious, on the other hand, is in constant motion.

It dreams unceasingly and follows its course below the surface of the conscious, like an underground stream. It is intimately connected with our vegetative functions. When we are aroused, or worried, our organism suffers the repercussions.

We are not, therefore, masters of our psychic life; in any case, not to the degree we suppose. We are being constantly invaded by emotional reactions, nightmares, imaginings, and depressions which are not under our control. We are continually receiving messages from the unconscious, the most significant of which are *dreams*. We speak or write one word for another; we make a gesture opposite to the one we want to make. These "flawed acts" of daily life, these messages, attest to the existence within us of an unknown region, which is outside our control.

The European mind, however, has difficulty in accepting this fact, and European males in particular suffer from a "tensing of the conscious"and an overestimation of their ability to be rational.

Some individuals identify integrally with their Persona.
They are conscious only of their social function; they are
little more than their outer mask : the functionary, the
clergyman, the military man, the actress, the woman of the
world, the professor, etc. They play their role by rote, and
their inner life is consequently impoverished. A striking
contrast may, however, exist between the way they represent
themselves in society and the way they act and behave in
private life. The statesman has fits of crying in secret, like
Bismarck, who was outwardly vigorous and tough in battle.
Others, on the contrary, are invaded, even submerged, by
their unconscious, to the point where they identify with their
own symbolic dramatis personae. This attitude, taken to the
extreme, leads to psychosis. (Jung, *La Dialectique entre le
Moi et l'Inconscient - The Relations between the Ego and the
Unconscious*).

The psyche, in its totality, is ruled by laws, the principal
one of which is *polarity*. The human soul is a self-regulating
energy system, but no state of equilibrium or any self-
governing system functions without inherent oppositions.
The contrast between the natural principle and the spiritual
principle, between instinct and mind, forms the basis of the
tension we call psychic energy or *libido*. This energy gives
the *intensity* of psychic activity. It has nothing to do with
moral, aesthetic or intellectual values, but is simply the
potential amount of energy available to the subject.

The *unconscious* and the *conscious* are in a *complementary* and *compensatory relation to each other*. Every
quality exaggerated in the conscious will be compensated, in
the unconscious, by its opposite. Every character element
that is weak or lacking in the outer personality will be found
in the unconscious attitude, serving as a counterweight. Thus,
an active person, sure of himself outside his family circle,
may be gentle and timid within it. A man tyrannical with his
subordinates, may be submissive to his wife. The barriers
between the two realms, rigid as they may appear, are only

relative, and the unconscious elements tend continually to rise above the threshold of the conscious.

We have already noted that two different layers have been identified in depth psychology, the *personal* or *individual unconscious* and the *collective or universal unconscious*. Flawed actions, moodiness, forgetfulness and complexes, which will be studied in depth further on, form a part of the personal unconscious. Nevertheless, we all carry inwardly, elements which have never been part of our conscious. Awareness or forgetfulness of these elements is not possible, as they have never risen into the conscious mind.

The *archetypal* images [1] common to mythology, to fairy tales and to our dreams, form the content of our collective unconscious. Man is heir to the treasures of every century. The collective unconscious is the maternal earth formed of age-old residues, into which the roots of the psyche reach down. They are the vestiges of ancient humanity, our common birthright.

The individual has evolved through the ages by a long process of differentiation, from a state of complete unconsciousness, in which where he was at one with all the elements of creation, to a more conscious state. All humanity follows this process, and each one of us achieves this in his life to a greater or lesser degree.

----

(1) The *Archetypes* are symbols of the human soul and its evolution, primordial images that have always existed and eternally persist. They should not be considered as the individual content of the psyche, but as dispositions. They are models, forms, so to speak, in which the individual's personal life is cast. We don't carry within us our experiences only, but also those of our ancestors, of the whole of humanity. Our unconscious has preserved these images, and reproduces them in our dreams, which thus often acquire an archaic and impersonal quality. (see Jung, *L'Homme et ses Sysmboles*, and A.Teillard, *Le Symbolisme de Rêve*).

The majority of human beings do not rise above the collective life. "All fundamental instincts and fundamental modes of thought and feeling are of a collective nature; likewise, all that is conventional and conformist. On closer scrutiny, it is amazing to see how much of what we believe to be part of our individual psychology is, in reality, wedded to collective feelings.... . Consequently, it is necessary to distinguish clearly between personal and collective assumptions. However, it is not always easy to discriminate between the two, for personal elements also derive from the collective psyche and are intimately bound up with it." (Jung: *La Dialectique entre le Moi et l'Inconscient - The Relations between the Ego and the Unconscious*).

The individual's close adherence to the collective psyche is of importance to the graphologist who, in his search for individual idiosyncrasies, so often encounters expressions of the collective life. The outward and conventional personality, which we call the "Persona," results from the conjunction of these two elements : the person who plays the role, and the collectivity that has vested it in him. A man becomes a general or a manufacturer because society has created these roles, but woe-betide him who refuses to play the game : society will take its revenge. An individual who assumes several roles simultaneously is already a bit suspect. We often doubt the competence of an employee who could double as a poet or a musician.

The graphologist who has just read these lines, has already pictured to himself types of handwriting that could be called "Persona handwritings". *Sacré-Coeur* writing, so frequent among women in high society, furnishes us with a perfect example of this, as do official calligraphy and some commercial handwritings.

Ex.1(a) and 1(b) - Persona Handwriting

These handwritings are the most difficult to analyse, precisely because of their imitative and thereby collective character. Individuality is hidden under appearances, sometimes stifled, or may even be non-existent.

The graphologist, who must choose the best secretary among some twenty typists, is sometimes more at a loss than when having to choose a gardener or a chambermaid. Indeed, it can be easier to analyse handwritings that are barely organised than it is to reveal the striking individual traits in a number of handwritings made uniform by a profession or calling.

It should be noted that the address produced on the envelope as well as the capital letters are particularly good indicators for graphologists of the outer personage. Pulver, in his book, *Die Symbolik der Handschrift*, gives particular attention to the address as an expression of the Persona. It is always interesting to study the interplay of compensations between the writer's outward attitude and his inner character.

All the representative exaggerations, such as those we see in artificial handwritings, imply reactions coming from the unconscious. It is not enough, therefore, in looking at the *Sacré-Coeur* writing, to note only the elegant and presumptuous attitude of a worldly woman, but to call attention to the small accessory signs that always appear and indicate inner conflicts such as timidity, fear, or other counterparts of the apparent attitude.

THE TYPES OF ATTITUDE :
EXTRAVERSION, INTROVERSION

> "The seat of the soul is where the inner world
> and the outer world touch each other."
>
> NOVALIS

Going back to the ideas of Heraclitus, analytical psychology sees life as a perpetual "becoming," an incessant opposition of positive and negative forces, a duality, a discordance, which should be dissolving or resolving into the invisible harmony of the great universal laws. All human law is but a pale imitation of divine law, just as our soul is nothing but a derivative of supreme reason. Separated from the latter, it is extinguished like a burning coal snatched from the hearth. Again, these oppositions may be found not only outside ourselves, but also within our soul; love and hate, attraction and repulsion, good and bad, life and death, justice and injustice, light and darkness. By their existence, they maintain balance in the world. The same ideas are found as well in Chinese and Hindu philosophy.

Character, therefore, can never be completely good or completely bad. It represents a play of more or less contradictory tendencies, obedient to laws that will be studied later.

Jung divides humanity into *two basic groups* : the group whose general attitude, interest and energy are principally directed outward : the *Extraverts* : and the group whose general attitude is directed principally inward : the *Introverts*.

These two attitudes are as old as civilisation itself. The introvert and the extravert are found in every period of history, and at all levels of human evolution, from the illiterate to the erudite, among primitive peoples as well as among the civilised.

The two psychological attitudes of introversion and extraversion do not represent two groups of human characters, as such, but, rather, psychic reactions that have become automatic to such a degree that they fix the type.

These reactions derive not only from the conscious domain, but also from the unconscious, in its compensatory role. The extraverted or introverted attitudes govern the totality of an individual's experiences. They exercise a predominant influence over relationships with one's fellow man and over one's development. This classification into two opposite types corresponds with Dr. Corman's psycho-morphological types, the *expanded* and the *contracted*; as well as, with Dr. Kretschmer's constitutional types, the *cyclothymes* and the *schizothymes*. William James, in his, *The Varieties of Religious Experience*, classified men into two categories that are equally analogous; the *tender-minded* man corresponding to the extravert, the *tough-minded* man to the introvert. Schiller, pursuant to his meetings with Goethe, spoke also of the nature of this antagonism between men, as being more divisive than questions of self-interest.

In the extravert, the libido is directed toward the outer world, that is to say, the object, while in the introvert, toward the inner world, that is to say, the subject. Goethe compared, the twofold movement of the psyche, either expanding or contracting to the diastolic or systolic movements of the heart which constituted a universal principle. For Jung, the diastole, the psychic exhalation, corresponds to extraversion, the systole, psychic inhalation, to introversion.

For the *extraverted* man, reaction toward the world of objects is spontaneous and immediate, whereas the *introverted* man's is hesitant and preceded by an inner contraction.

Diverse action, events of the present moment, assume a principal importance in the life of the former. People and things are of infinite interest to him and he adapts quickly and easily. Made for social life, he thinks and acts in conformity with the demands of his world, professing the opinions and judgements of his time and place.

He detests solitude. His interests, his attention are completely turned toward the outside. The exterior life interests him profoundly. He expends himself on it, hurls himself unreservedly into it. His nature is extensive, but not intensive; for, while he enters easily into relations with his circle, he cannot orientate himself with ease toward the inner world, sometimes even denies or is unaware of its existence. He considers as useless and morbid all preoccupation with the subject of his own ego and generally appears well balanced, because he deals with circumstances effortlessly. But, this easy adaptation often hides an inner void and sometimes conceals a flight from life. In its exaggerated form, extraversion leads to a neurosis: *hysteria*.

The extravert is therefore companionable and provides a liaising element. Without him, introverts would remain in their shell, never making contact with others. But the introvert, for his part, is the guardian of the inner world.

The *introvert* is, broadly speaking, the opposite of the extravert. For him, the importance of the object does not reside in the object itself, but in the value he attributes to it. It is not the situation, taken objectively, that is important, but the situation as he sees it. His interests are fundamentally based on his subjective view; that is why he is often seen as egoistic and egocentric. Such judgements are superficial, for neither the introvert nor the extravert has a monopoly on egoism.

If the extravert, more sparkling, more personable and easy to fathom, charms at the outset he does not always withstand the test of deeper acquaintanceship. The introvert, on the contrary is more private, but gains on further acquaintance.

The introvert is often timid, awkward. He is withdrawn in himself and fears the impressions that come to him from the outside. As he reserves his personal opinions, others may not understand him, thereby isolating him. Entrenched in his inner life, he lives in dreams and speculations in a world of his own. He lacks the flexibility and adaptability of the opposite type, but possesses a greater depth of feeling and thought.

When difficulties arise, a conflict, a drama, the reaction of the two types will again be different: the extravert will mingle with the crowd, seeking forgetfulness in distractions and sensations: the introvert, on the other hand, will take refuge in a profound withdrawal. These differences of reaction are manifested in all human relationships: between children and parents, and especially in the sentimental life, between lovers and spouses. *The extravert fears losing contact, the introvert fears conflict.*

Exaggerated introversion leads to *obsessional neurosis*, and in psychiatric cases, to *schizophrenia*.

The two basic attitudes just described are not the result of either the social milieu or of education; in the same family, one of the children may be extraverted, and the other introverted. But the influence of the *milieu* can impede a child's development, push him into an attitude which is not natural to him. An hysterical mother through excessive displays of affection, can unconsciously force her child into an introverted attitude. The timid scholar, withdrawn from the world, can provide his son with an example of such awkwardness that the latter assumes a contradictory attitude of excessive extraversion.

However, *there reside in every person both possibilities of orientation*. The same individual can be more introverted during certain periods of his life, and more extraverted in others. The adolescent almost always goes through a phase of introversion before opening himself up to love. One historical period can be more marked than another by one of these two attitudes. Our era is extraverted. The Middle Ages were introverted.

The movement of the two attitudes is like that of a pendulum swinging in one direction, then in the other. But, despite these fluctuations, one of the two will always predominate, thus deciding the type.

In our day, Westerners are more apt to appreciate extraversion than introversion; to have a social or political ideal, an interest in mechanics, in hygiene and in progress, or in all activities which seem to him to be healthy and legitimate. For the Hindu, on the contrary, the essential aim of life lies in introspection and meditation.

The psychologist knows that withdrawal into the self is as indispensable as the drive toward the outside world and, more and more, the masters of the intellectual and spiritual life emphasise the necessity for an inner life. John Layard, in his book, *The Lady of the Hare*, expresses a desire to see analytical psychology, rich in its recent experiences, collaborating intimately, someday, with philosophy, medicine and religion to create a *science of introversion*, which would lead us to a deeper understanding of the human soul.

Introversion is often confused with egocentrism, extraversion with altruism. But, in reality, it is a matter of the two opposite directions that the libido can take. When the introvert turns away from the world to retire into himself, he finds not only his Ego, but another universe[1]. Introspection, by way of the Ego, leads to another world peopled with spiritual objects. What does the mystic seek, if not his God? And the Hindu or Tibetan Yogi, who hunches over the Mandala, the votive image, pursues, through his meditations, an inner voyage the goal of which is union with Brahma, the Supreme Being, the "All".

Introversion, as well as extraversion, can lead either to inflation or detachment of the personal Ego.

It is perhaps through the function of Intuition that the fundamental essence of introversion is easiest to understand. *Intueri* means, to contemplate. What the introvert regards or contemplates is not his Ego, but the animate and inexhaustible world of the unconscious; and, beyond that, other worlds. The practice of introspection permits us to increase our psychic capacities, to awaken in us the so-called "supernatural" faculties such as clairvoyance, clairaudience, all of which belong to the domain of introversion.

While the introvert lives "on the moon", unable to adapt to material contingencies, the extravert remains a stranger to the inner world. Away from visible realities, he can feel as helpless as the introvert can feel at a market or in a large store. It is as difficult for the one as for the other to deviate from their natural attitude. But, to a great degree, the art of life consists in achieving a rhythmic movement between extraversion and introversion.

The foregoing sheds light only on a single aspect of the matter : *the conscious attitude of the two types.*

---

(1) On this subject, read : George Du Maurier, *Peter Ibbetson* (Pub., Gallimard) and A.Teillard, *La Dimension Inconnue* (Pub. Baconnière, Neuchâtel).

The reactions of the unconscious are generally opposed to those of the conscious. Thus, the unconscious of the extravert type is introverted, and vice versa. We will look at this problem more closely when studying the psychological functions. Essentially, however, the predominant attitude, in other words, the conscious attitude (which decides the type) is always more spontaneous, more positive and more constructive than the other. The unconscious attitude, being opposed, is often infantile and primitive. These inner contradictions create tensions, conflicts and even neuroses.

Two methods of exploration bring to light the movement of the libido : they are *psychoanalysis* and *graphology*.

The first one follows the transformations of the libido through the medium of dreams. There, the tendencies, the functions, the character traits are represented by people, animals and objects of the dream life [1]. Graphology explores these transformations through the scriptural movement frozen on paper. These two methods complement and confirm one another.

Transformation of handwriting in the course of psychoanalytical treatment

Psychoanalysis re-establishes the continuity between these apparently unrelated and often contradictory pheno-mena and grasps the intermediary links that allow an understanding of the progressive displacements from one tendency to another. Observation of the same individual's

---

(1) See: C.G.Jung. *L'Homme à la Découverte de son Ame, Métamorphose de l'Ame et ses Symboles,* Charles Bauduin, *Introduction à l'Analyse des Rêves* and A.Teillard, *Le Symbole du Rêve, Le Rêve, une Porte sur le Réel.*.

handwriting, during different periods of his life, also permits us to evaluate these changes in the modifications of the graphic trail. I have studied the handwriting of different subjects in the course of psychoanalytical treatment. The transformations were clearly inscribed in the dynamism of the writing trail. I offer some examples of this. Hand-writing has here the advantage of fixing the movement of the libido.

Sometimes, for example, the over-expanded, manifestly unstructured handwritings of hysterics become contracted, while the rigid handwritings of obsessives expand and become more flexible. The two kinds of handwritings thus lose their usual exaggerated characteristics, to approach in consequence more normal and harmonious handwriting.

However, I observed, furthermore, that the handwritings of those subjects analysed by a doctor manifested a diminution of personality. These handwritings became bland, fearful, expressionless, and revealed a general enfeeblement. The doctor-analyst was dismayed by these observations.

The substitution of the analyst's personality for that of his patients, provoked in them a regression of the libido.

It has been known, for a long time, that handwriting reflects not only an individual's physiological development, but also his psychological development. Still, one must remember that handwriting does not always closely follow the rhythm of these developments. In general the *transformation of a handwriting comes after changes in the personality*, but there are cases where future transformations, not yet evident in behaviour, are manifested first in the handwriting.

Our first example of transformation in a handwriting during the course of analytical treatment, shows the change of direction of the libido and, in its train, a transformation of character and behaviour in a positive sense. The two specimens come from a 19 year old girl, and were taken at the beginning and the end of an instructive analysis that lasted almost a year and a half. The person analysed wanted this experience to serve as a basis for future graphological studies.

Ex. 2. - Before analysis

Ex. 3. - After analysis. Transformation of a writing
in the course of psychoanalytical treatment, following
C.G.Jung's synthetic method.

The first, and unexpected, effect of the analysis was a transformation of character, which was markedly shown in the writing. The writer was an introvert, cold, shut-in, lacking spontaneous contact with her surroundings. After several months of intense work with her, the psychic energy turned away from her personal Ego and effected a rightward movement toward the world [1]. The writing became larger, the arcades changed into angular garlands, and the disconnected and left-slanted writing became more connected and progressive. The childish character of the writing, before treatment, was changed into a more mature and expressive writing. Several characteristics, such as the large spaces between words, have remained (contact with her surroundings being difficult), but the spaces between lines have become larger, that is to say, there is greater clarity of thought. The writer will never lose her basic character, that of an introvert, but the movement of the libido has expanded and the outside world, thanks to the increase in extraversion she was able to achieve, has become more accessible to her.

Obviously, we are dealing here with a very young person and the evolution registered in her handwriting is, on the one hand, facilitated by the subject's youth and on the other hand, by her ardent desire to perfect herself. There are other cases in which the individual's transformation, attained by an inner struggle, became exteriorised only much later.

2nd case : a 25 year-old Frenchman, a philosophy student. This young man, who put several writing specimens at my disposal, from among which I chose the most striking, also provided the following detailed remarks:

"My analysis lasted about twenty months, from January 1945 to September 1946. I had met Madeleine in September 1943. A great love bound us together and we were married.

---

(1) See the chapter on the *Symbolism of Space*. See the explanation of technical terms in the graphological Dictionary.

At the end of 1944, a crisis broke out. Madeleine turned away from me, she hesitated, then her whole love for me was brought into question. Total collapse for me. I managed to overcome her denial of any sexual relations, but not her inhibition. No longer any hope.

thèse de droit pénal sur « la récidive » inspirée de l'école criminelle positive. Condamné pour c d suite d'un discours du 5 juin 1916 — En 1916 secret d cipaliste socialiste — Élu député en 1919_1921_1926 fuite en octobre 1922 examiné par les sicaires de Mussolini

Ex. 4. - Handwriting before beginning psychoanalytical treatment, according to the method of Freud.
(1st document of 1938).

"Before this crisis, I had turned to psychoanalysis. One day I saw an analyst, who diagnosed extensive narcissism and recommended analysis.

"My analysis brought out not only narcissism but also latent homosexuality : fixation on my brother.

"Improvement appeared really only at the end of the analysis, several months later. It began with the reversal of the love situation that had appeared irreparably compromised. I succeeded in getting Madeleine to accept sex, which rid her of all her inhibitions in this matter, and we began on a firmer basis of reality. I am now basically involved in an objective way and I have rid myself of my brother's intellectual and spiritual tutelage. I feel more at ease with a greater readiness for life and can assert myself with a more responsive manliness and also greater aggressiveness."

Diagnosis from the handwritings

1st Specimen 1938. A writing that is small, regular, monotonous, left-slanted, juxtaposed, fine and artificial, rigid, with harsh angles, sometimes semi-arcaded, indicating great inhibitions and repression, resulting in timidity and difficulty with free expression in life. The writer is introverted, without finding the necessary compensation in a movement toward the world. He lacks expansiveness, he doesn't give of himself. The libido is blocked, fixated at an infantile stage. The diagnosis of narcissism is confirmed by study of the writing. To that must be added a overexclusive introversion. Concentration on the personal (or empirical) Ego. Intel-ligence is good, but blocked. There is sensitivity, but feeling is not expressed. The writer is cut off from the resources of his unconscious. He is psychologically anaemic.

méprise le démon et je n' ai qu' une de vous rester étroitement unie et de x avec le secours de votre grâce. que le d' impureté par la très pure virginité

Ex. 5. - Change in the handwriting in the course of psychoanalytical treatment. (2nd document).

The 2nd Specimen dates from 1944 (after marriage). The writing has evolved. It is more natural, more released from inhibitions. It indicates an awakening of the emotive life and the beginning of a mobilisation of energy.

The 3rd Specimen dates from 1946 (after the end of treatment). Here, a change is clearly affirmed. The writing is larger than the preceding one. It is more subtly nuanced, more ventilated, the letter forms are richer, more expressive. The general level has been raised. The writing has also become more irregular. This isn't always a sign of development; but, in this young man, the unevenness indicates a liberation of energies and particularly of emotivity, until now curbed and repressed. He achieves an easier expression of his whole personality.

ont fort de considérer qu'a correspond un ordre de phénom Ce n'est pas su but mon avis

Ex. 6. - Change in the handwriting in the course of psychoanalytical treatment. (3rd document).

The writing has retained its disconnected, vertical, slightly artificial character. Development is beginning. The writer is young : he still has much to do, especially in the area of feeling. Analysis has opened up to him a way in which his energy, finally freed, can be discharged.

As to the psychological type, the writer is without doubt an *introvert*, and he will always retain his basic character. His principal function [1] is Intuition. One might hesitate between Intuition-Thinking and Thinking-Intuition in classifying him, but the preference is for the first pair, because the reality sense, the Sensation function (the opposite of Intuition), is his inferior function, even more than Feeling, which yields the following diagram :

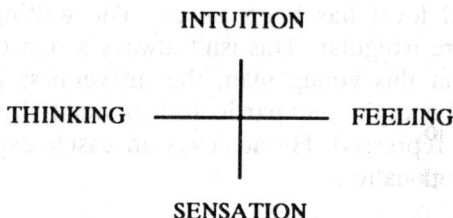

$$\text{INTUITION}$$

$$\text{THINKING} \quad \text{------} \quad \text{FEELING}$$

$$\text{SENSATION}$$

If we compare the first and third specimens, we can see that Intuition has been freed from the grip of Thinking, to which the writer during the first period, clung in a movement of agonised fear. He therefore was not living according to his best function, Intuition, but with the help of his auxiliary function, Thinking. Many of his difficulties in the area of love, therefore, in his relations with another person, certainly came from his poorly differentiated Feeling function, which he will be able to render conscious and develop, as he has done for his Intuition.

A vast field of exploration is open to collaboration between the graphologist and psychologist, on the condition, however, that both sides speak the same language.

The matter has been very difficult until now, because of the often inexact and subjective terminology of graphologists and the isolated position that graphology held. I would be

---

(1) I am anticipating the study of the functions further on, p.76.

happy if the present work is able to contribute to a reconciliation of the two methods [1].

Extraversion and Introversion and their Expression in Handwriting

The handwriting of the extravert type is principally characterised by a *tendency to expansion* : i.e., by its amplitude, its centrifugal movement, its rightward tendency, its prolongations upward and downward.

On the other hand, *the handwriting of the introvert* is, overall, more compressed, *more concentrated, demanding less space.*

In general, *extraversion* produces a variability of forms in the writing trail, while *introversion* creates greater sobriety. In the graphic expression of the psychological functions, introverted Thinking and Intuition, produce a great richness of forms, but in an intensive, not extensive way. Therefore, this *variety of forms*, will be manifested in a *small writing*. The introvert flees from all showy exteriorisation. In general, he seeks simplification. Being, by nature, limited in his potentialities for exteriorisation, his writing quite naturally reflects this same characteristic of discretion.

---

(1) Such collaboration between psychoanalysts and graphologists has now been achieved in several countries. Unhappily, it is very difficult to publish the results obtained, due to professional secrecy.

Several younger graphologists have felt the necessity of undergoing the experience of psychoanalysis: on the one hand, to explore their own depths and eventually to free themselves from their complexes; and, on the other hand, to understand thoroughly the meaning of the analytical terminology they use in their work.

I can only congratulate them on their enterprise which, in any case, signifies an opening up of the unconscious, a broadening of the personality and a wider perception of the problems.

Ex. 7. - Extraversion

Ex. 8. - Extraversion.

Attitudes as complex as extraversion and introversion obviously cannot be expressed by a simple, isolated sign, a single trait, but by an *ensemble of signs,* by groups of signs or syndromes.The characteristic signs mentioned in the following tables *have no value on their own, but only in combination with one another*. It goes without saying that these signs do not all appear together. They way in which they are assembled can be different each time, but on their own do not have the same degree of importance.

Ex. 9. - Hysteria, sexual complexes

It must be repeated in this context, that every individual has both mechanisms : extraversion and introversion. There is neither a pure extravert, nor a pure introvert, but one of these attitudes is always predominant and it is necessary to discover the play of the two tendencies in the handwriting.

Graphic expression of extraversion

Generosity in the layout : wide margins
Right-tending, (progressive)
Large
Expanded, spread out
Right-slanted
Angular garlands (when the writing is large)
Large garlands, right-slanted and expanded
Precipitate, dynamically stimulated (*)
Increasing left margin
Ample
Prolonged upward and downward
Lines rising, or variable in direction
Enlarging
Accents or t-bars ahead of the text
Finals in open curves
Large, centrifugal t-bars and f-bars
Thrown
Lower extensions in the form of large triangles
Signature placed to the right
Signature large
Address placed on the right side of the envelope

(*) "Dynamically stimulated" poorly translates the French term (*dynamogeniée*), which includes the idea of simplification and rightward drive of increasing intensity that is energised effortlessly from within.

Extraversion with a tendency to hysteria

(A) Very large writing
Predominant middle zone
Exaggeration of all the forms
Artificial
Embellished
Spasmodic, with irregular pressure
Exaggerated underlining
Exaggerated punctuation (exclamation marks)
Displaced pressure (on the upstrokes)

All the general characteristics of the handwritings of extraverts are found, in exaggerated form, in the handwriting of hysterical people.

Ex. 10. - Extraversion with a tendency to hysteria

Ex. 11. - Hysteria

(B) *Other manifestations of extraversion with a*
    tendency to hysteria :

    Exaggeration of the forms, but at the same time,
    dissolving into a weak, thready handwriting.

Thus, there are several types of handwriting showing
hysterical tendencies : on the one hand, large, artificial
ostentatious handwritings and, on the other hand, extremely
thready handwritings becoming formless.

Pressure varies according to the degree of vitality. One
may find very different pressures in the same type of
attitude. Pressure is therefore separate from the graphic
expression of extraversion or introversion.

Graphic expression of introversion

Economy in layout
Sober, contained
Small
Squeezed
Vertical or slightly right-slanted
Thin
Arcaded or in small garlands
Simplified
Margins rather tight, cramped
Decreasing left margin
Large spaces between words (especially with
narrow writing)
Upper extension of the "d" curved leftward (the
lyrical "d")
Short finals
T-bars to the left of the letter
Address placed toward the left
Signature placed to the left
Signature small, without paraph
Signature followed by a full stop
Typographic layout

Introversion with a tendency to obsession

All the general characteristics of introversion are found,
in exaggerated form, in the handwriting of obsessive
neurotics.

Mechanical, monotonous, automatic
Very small
Very narrow
Extremely thin
Simultaneously small, narrow and muddy
Inhibited

une note n votre proposition

r, avec mes. remerciements pour la
nikotry à mon égard, l'expression n mes

Gabriel Ornano

Ex. 12. - Introversion

Je vous souhaite bonnes
vacances ! à la Charlotte, et
Charente
     Recevez, cher Monsieur,
mon cordial souvenir

Marie Noël

Ex. 12 (a). - Introversion

Amended
Sacré-Coeur type, very narrow
Drooping at the ends of lines.
Short finals, or with needlepoints
Lines very horizontal and parallel
Signature followed by a full stop or encircled
by a leftward curve
Signature reduced to initials and placed to the left
under the text

Ex. 13. - Introversion. Obsessional neurosis. Anal complex.

Ex. 13(a). - Introversion. Obsessional ideas.

The two main directions the libido can take, extraversion and introversion, play a very important role in the different *ages of one's life.*

The child, in his first years of life, displays a remarkable will to make contact with the world around him and adapt to its conditions. It is this almost exclusively extraverted attitude which allows this conquest and assimilation.

Adolescence, on the contrary, is the age of introversion, at least transitorily. The young man withdraws into himself (see the chapter on *The Formation of Character*), but soon he is obliged to come out of his shell in order to pursue his studies, or make his way in life. If this adjustment of energy does not take place, if the adolescent does not manage to break away from the paternal home, and particularly from his mother's influence, and create a life of his own, defeat and discouragement will be inevitable, often followed by neuroses.

In the first half of his life, up to about thirty-five or forty, man takes his place in the real world, in society. He develops his body, gathers knowledge, embraces a career, and starts a family. His attitude is generally all one of hope for the future. His libido is in a state of *progression.*

In the second half of life, past the peak point, the curve descends and this new direction demands another adjustment of the libido, since his duties change, or modify, in the course of time. It is no longer a matter of concern to him to preserve the species or the race, but a question of a duty towards himself, which requires *introversion.*

Once again, an adjustment of psychic energy is necessary, when a man must prepare himself for his separation from life. He must detach his libido from the objects and people around him. If he does not succeed in this, a regression of the libido will occur and we see the neuroses of the elderly appear: fear, inferiority complex, a feeling of emptiness and, especially, a painful feeling of absolute uselessness.

Life, through its natural evolution, from its dawn to its dusk, forces us into a continual adjustment of our libido. "Life represents an energy *processus*, essentially irreversible and consequently directed toward a single end, the state of rest. As the projectile's trajectory ends at its designated point, so life ends in death, which is similarly the final point of the trajectory of life. Even its ascent and arrival at the culminating point are simply stages, a means of reaching the goal; in other words, death." (Jung, *Wirklichkeit der Seele*).

Thus Jung, as a psychologist and doctor, urges all those who seek his advice, in this critical transition from maturity to old age, to cultivate their metaphysical or religious tendencies, for they alone can give meaning to the end of life.

The supreme task of the man in the later stages of life is *individuation*. It is at this time he must become aware of his inner being, when, thanks to that awareness, he can flow with a spiritual tide that permits him a new progression of his psychic energy.

So, at the onset of the second phase of life, by developing a profound introversion, we pass through a second adolescence; a new phase expressed by a youthfulness that comes to us from within. The first part of life is more favourable to extraversion, while quite often it is only in maturity that the introvert finally feels happy and in his element.

The Hindus and the Chinese have known about Yoga, the royal art of introversion, for millennia. The great mystics of the European Middle Ages lived in deep introspection and meditation. Our era has discovered ways that are analogous to the ancient practices : for us, introversion crosses over into the search for the unconscious.

PSYCHIC ENERGY AND ITS EVOLUTION

Until now we have considered the human soul in a rather static way, much like a three-storey building in which the conscious is represented by the upper storey, the personal or individual unconscious by the middle storey, and the collective unconscious by the building's foundations, which are sunk into the earth and become part of it. Now, we are going to consider the soul in its dynamic aspect, as an *energy system.*

Analytical psychology sees the human soul as an ensemble of functions determining the individual's adaptation to the conditions of the milieu in which he evolves; and, in a parallel way, to the conditions of his inner structure. It is a psychic energy system governed by laws comparable to those that govern a physical energy system. Using Jung's work, *On Psychic Energy,* as the main source of reference, from which his definition of psychic energy, or *libido*, has already been quoted, this is not for him, as it was for Freud, specifically sexual. It is equivalent to the totality of energy, of which sexuality is but a part. There are no ethical, aesthetic or intellectual implications. "The intensity of psychic activity can only be evaluated through its manifestations and its effects".

One of the fundamental laws it obeys is that of the *conservation of energy*.

Indeed, the quality of the disposable psychic energy can change in the course of the energy *processus*, but its quantity remains invariable. Whether it is manifested in the conscious area, or in the unconscious; whether it develops in the form of practical, intellectual and artistic activity, or in the form of dreams, throughout all its transformations, its quantity remains constant.

Let us take for example, a woman who passionately loves her husband, or her child, and loses the object of her affections. Her psychic energy, having been totally utilised in that love, will now fall into a vacuum. What will the wife, or the mother, do with this ever-present, but suddenly purposeless energy? She has several possibilities open to her, but the fact remains that her fund of energy will need to find an outlet, one way or another. A new love object must be found, or another activity. Failing this, the libido could develop into a neurosis, or even a physical illness [1].

Distractions, such as travelling, are superficial ways to help in the redirection of the libido. They serve to create a bridge between the two different stages, but are not enough for complete regeneration. The transformation of energy must occur at the core of the individual, and not just superficially.

A man, whose profession is the pivotal point of his life, may feel seriously upset when he is obliged to discontinue his professional activity; for example, when he has to retire. The psychic energy, for years channelled in the same groove, has nowhere to go. It is not unusual for a professor, military man,

---

(1) See also: Charles Baudouin, *La Mobilisation de l'Energie*.

manufacturer or merchant, suddenly retired from business, to become an unbearable domestic tyrant subject to depressions from which he has never suffered before.

A truly absorbing interest is the only thing that can save him. Happy is the man who, through a secondary interest outside his profession, has had the foresight to prepare for this inevitable situation.

The movement of psychic energy is either *progressive* or *regressive*. *Progression* represents a permanent effort at adaptation to the outside environment, which life demands. However, we cannot, in the long run be equal to these demands if we have failed to adapt to the conditions of the inner life, if we are not in harmony with ourselves.

Regression, on the contrary, is a refusal to carry out this effort. The regressive attitude is disastrous and unhealthy, however, only if it becomes permanent. At certain periods of life, a transitory regression is essential. "One must first recoil the better to jump".

Our psychic life continually oscillates between two poles. Here, again, progression and regression of the libido represent the two opposite attitudes necessary for the human being's development. If one attitude is developed to the extreme, or adopted to the exclusion of the other, it will inevitably provoke a contrary reaction.

With regard to the structure of the psyche, the regulatory function of the unconscious has already been pointed out. The opposing unconscious pole of necessity reacts to all exaggerations of the conscious pole. For example, a puritanical or ascetic attitude, pushed to the extreme, elicits dreams and visions of an excessive sensuality (see the *Temptation of St. Anthony*, by the Flemish master, Jerome Bosch). Earlier, Heraclitus taught that everything, having reached its zenith, is transformed into its opposite. This is the law of alternation and reversal of effects, a law common to all biological reactions.

Psychic energy can be expressed with infinite variety, in social relationships, in the intellectual or practical sphere, in all manual occupations, artistic or otherwise. It can be directed outward or inward. When the libido is orientated toward the inner life, it animates imaginative or mystical centres of energies previously unknown to the subject (conversions and poetic revelations hitherto in captivity). If the libido is directed outward, it is transformed into activity. A man's *will* is psychic energy consciously directed towards a goal.

Let us now describe some of its characteristic attitudes :

The progressive attitude of the libido is accompanied by feelings and sensations of energy, of well-being and hope. One feels able to face up to the exigencies of life : it is the present moment and the future that count, rather than preoccupation with the past. It is a state of mobilisation of all the vital energies, it is the feeling of the man who has confidence in himself and in life. This positive and dynamic condition gives confidence to others and attracts success. It is by this mobilisation of energy, by this ordering of activity that we seek to discipline the will in all sorts of ways. Physical health also profits from this harmony and this dynamism.

The regressive attitude has an entirely different aspect. It is a state of fatigue, of depression, of discouragement, in which one lacks interest in life. The smallest difficulties seem like insurmountable peaks : one is apprehensive of the slightest changes in one's life. The individual recoils before any effort : he feels inferior. He fears risks and in his mind turns away from the present to take refuge in the past. This general diminution of the personality leads, perforce, to disappointment and defeat. One can neither convince others nor inspire confidence in them when one is in a regressive condition.

Finally, a third state, as painful as the preceding one, if not more difficult to bear, even when transitory, is *blockage* of the libido.

That will be the case, for example, with someone who, having got completely bogged down, cannot find in himself either the courage or a way of extricating himself from his difficulties. Without going to the extreme, many people remain in a state of aridity, of boredom, of need, because they don't have the necessary enthusiasm to climb out of their rut. The vital *processus* requires a continual adjustment of energy, a constant process of living and dying.

The psychologist, who observes and follows the destiny of many people, knows the power of the libido's influence over the outer life. He knows that the slightest progressive movement of the libido always elicits a "response" from life: sometimes, it can be another person's unexpected reactions, sometimes a latent energy needing only to be released to realise one's possibilities.

Almost all neuroses have a more or less regressive character. The neurotic is tied to his childhood memories : he recoils from the slightest difficulty, and has lost his taste for life. One of the goals of analytical treatment is to find in the subject's unconscious, through his dreams and complexes, a vital interest, a living spark capable of kindling his smothered psyche. Regression, which may become chronic in certain neuroses, can then give way to a progressive condition, with a new mobilisation of energy.

The collective unconscious is the inexhaustible source from which proceeds the dynamism of the psychic life, called libido, which manifests itself with as much variety as life itself and which is susceptible to as many successive transformations as physical energy. If nothing occurs to create an obstacle to the supply, this surge of energy will flow freely through the channels of the natural tendencies. But, if a traumatic experience occurs which, like a foreign body, obstructs the flow of the libido anywhere in its course, then blockage, complexes, repression and regression are produced.

The pictorial and sculptural representations of the libido are many, from earliest times down to the present.

One of the classic images, which also appears in our dreams, is the *horse*. The horse that carries man, be it savage and spirited, or well behaved and domesticated, perfectly expresses psychic energy in its varied forms : unbridled or controlled energy. Winged like Pegasus, the horse is the symbol of free, creative energy. In myths and fairy tales, horses are endowed with supernatural faculties. They understand human language, they speak, they herald danger and death.

Another of the libido's great symbols is the *river*. Like our psychic energies, it flows freely, bestowing life and fertility : or, when swollen and unleashed, it inundates everything around it.

The images representative of the libido are innumerable and in our nocturnal life, we imbibe of these symbolic reservoirs in which the traces of times past are mingled with the images of modern life [1].

The dynamic conception of the soul is interesting to the graphologist, for the libido is likewise registered in handwriting, which, in its essence, is dynamic. The scriptural movement follows with the greatest fidelity, the libido's fluctuations.

The intensity of the writing will show the writer's vitality and psychic élan. The flexibility will show the degree of

---

(1) I refer those of our readers to whom these questions are of interest, to the following works: Jung, *Métamorphoses de l'Ame et ses Symboles, L'Homme à la Découverte de son Ame, Le Moi et l'Inconscient*, and my *Symbolisme de Rêve*.

adaptability to the outside world and the direction will show the subject's tendencies and aspirations. We can say that *there is not only a pictorial and sculptural representation, but a scriptural representation of the libido.*

Ex. 14. - *Bismarck's signature*

Analytical psychology has defined *dreams* as a *self-representation of the libido. Handwriting is another form of self-representation of this same energy.*

Let us, however, note that the problem of handwriting is complicated by the fact that conscious elements intermingle with unconscious elements during the act of writing [1].

_____

(1) See : Magnat, *Poésie de l'Ecriture*

Expression of the Libido in Handwriting

A psychological assumption of such importance cannot be explained by an isolated sign, or even by a single group of signs, but it has a mode of expression that influences the whole writing trail and impregnates it with its essence. In fact, the libido, its intensity and its course are expressed in a very visible way through several graphic manifestations. The whole dynamism of the writing depends on the intensity of the libido, which is principally expressed through pressure.

Following are the signs discovered up to the present which can be grouped in a number of ways :

Expression of a strong libido

Firm, strong pressure
Large
In relief
Regular
Dynamically stimulated [*]
Rhythmic
Stability and unity of the writing trail
Precision of forms, especially in the "m's", "n's" and "u's"
Well developed and regular lower extensions
Angular
Heavy
Precise
Well nourished
Pasty

(*) Refer to footnote, page 50, and keep it in mind.

Expression of a weak libido

Light
Pale
Irregular
Unstable
Weak or thready
Monotonous
Extremely small
Descending lines
Stepped or undulating lines
Lower extensions :
    Abortive, inconsistent
    Looped down low
    Unlooped
    Skidding leftward
Low
Shaky
Diminishing
Right slanted at an angle of less than 45 degrees
Blurred
Very juxtaposed, fragmented
Slack
Suspended

Ex. 15. - *Strong libido*

*Monsieur je termi
en vous demandant c
en attendant je contim
les médicaments ordon*

Ex. 16. - *Weak libido*

*moi quelques vieilles robes
anciennes qui pourront me
pour quelques ouvrages j'a
suite gagné la sympathie
mieux j'aime mieux pla*

Ex. 16 (a). - *Weak libido*

Progressive attitude of the libido

Rhythmic
Dynamically stimulated
Harmonious
In relief, regular
Rapid, precipitated
Thrown
Grouped

Progressive
Expanded
Rising lines
Accent placed high and ahead of the text
Signature placed to the right
Enlarging left margin

Regressive attitude of the libido

Monotonous
Regressive
Squeezed
Extremely small
Weak and atrophied lower extensions
Left-slanted
Inhibited
Slow
Slack
Descending lines, descending tiles
Unfinished letters
Twisted letters
T-bars absent or placed very low
Signature placed to the left and lacking vigour

Observation. - It is especially difficult to uncover the graphic expression of *regression* due to the innate complexity of the problem. The state of regression can be expressed by an individual in many ways : by exaggerated expansiveness, or a flight from the world. Any great sorrow in life, or a defeat, can set in motion either a state of passivity, of brooding about oneself, or melancholy, or an exaggerated need for distractions, or a desire to get tipsy; all forms of regression that may have different and even opposite reflections in the handwriting.

An artificial and complicated handwriting may disguise a state of regression.

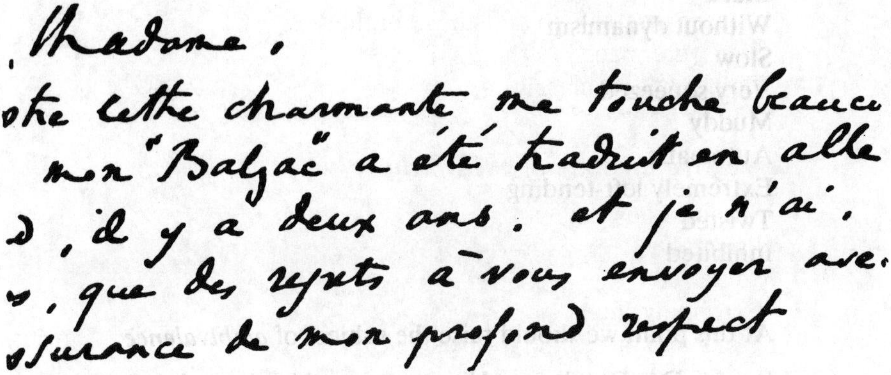
Madame,
otre lettre charmante me touche beauco
mon "Balzac" a été traduit en alle
, il y a deux ans. et je n'ai
, que des regrets à vous envoyer ave
ssurance de mon profond respect

Ex. 17. - *Libido in progression*

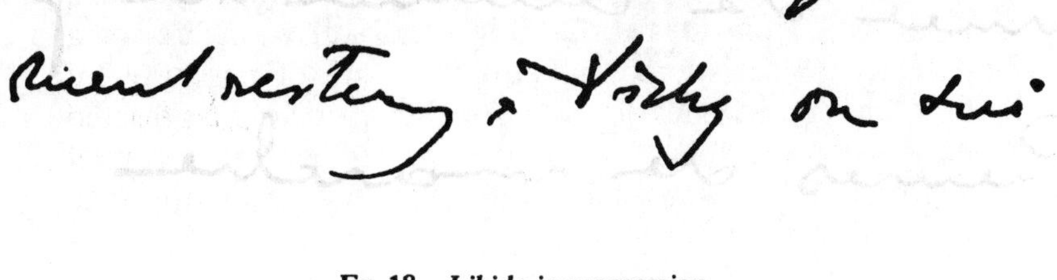
que la Banque
à Marseille. - Est-ce que vous
resterez à Vichy ou

Ex. 18. - *Libido in progression*

Expression of a blocked libido

Thick
Black
Without dynamism
Slow
Very squeezed
Muddy
Automatic
Extremely left-tending
Twisted
Inhibited

At this point we should raise the subject of *ambivalence*.

It was Dr. Bleuler, a Viennese psychiatrist, who first exposed the scope of the problem of ambivalence (*Lehrbuch der Psychiatrie*, Springer, Berlin, 1923). Ambivalence is seen in two contradictory attitudes that exist simultaneously in the same psyche : love and hate, attraction and revulsion, desire and fear, etc., in the face of a particular situation. The normal

Ex. 19. - *Libido in regression*

encore démenti depuis 8 jours.
aux orteils : l'une a complétera
de sa cicatrision. Restent encore
et dans toute la jambe inférieu

Ex. 20. - Libido in regression

chère madame,

Ex. 21. - **Strong libido, but blocked**

person understands this condition which today is referred to as "conflict". It is often at the root of the problem of indecisive, fugitive characters who run away from responsibilities. Many neurotics never achieve action because of an almost permanent state of ambivalence. Pushed to the extreme, this leads to a dissociation of personality that can be observed in certain mental illnesses such as schizophrenia.

The normal person reconciles these conflicting tendencies more or less easily, but the sick person, is invaded and torn apart by them. Stevenson's famous novel, *Dr. Jekyll and Mr. Hyde*, illustrates this dissociation of the personality into its two opposite poles : the faultless person and the despicable person, a dissociation that pushes the hero into hopelessness and crime.

Ex. 22. - Ambivalence

Graphic expression of Ambivalence

Changes of direction, particularly in the middle zone
Variably slanted
Variations in the length of the lower extensions
An exaggerated Sacré-Coeur style of writing
Angular, rigid writing
Sudden stops in continuity

(See also : Max Pulver, *Graphologia*, 1938/1)

The Will and its Expression in Handwriting

The *will* is considered by modern psychology as part of the universal energy that makes up our life. It directs our psychic functions and charges them with energy. It is the sum of the psychic energy at the disposal of the conscious. The will is one of humanity's recent acquisitions : it is unknown to animals or to primitive men, who are moved by instinct. Keyerling describes this condition very nicely in his *Méditations Sud-Américaines*. If "Gana" (desire) does not impel him, the primitive abstains from action. When a savage tribe wants to go off to war, it performs a war dance in order to stimulate energy and put the men in a state of collective exaltation. Imagination has to be set in motion by means of masks and symbolic gestures, so as to awaken the libido from its passive state.

The will sets in motion elements which surge up from the unconscious. For us, also, imagination stimulates our will. Coué demonstrated, that in the battle between will and imagination, it is the imagination which prevails.

The will is often symbolised in dreams by weapons and tools. It is interesting to note that, in handwriting, too, the will is expressed by clubbed or sharp-pointed horizontal strokes resembling weapons. It is particularly the aggressive will, turned combative and charged with affectivity, which takes these forms.

Graphic expression of the will

Will power always presupposes a conscious act. It is the libido directed toward a goal.

Regular
Dynamically stimulated
Firm
Poised
Thrown, flying strokes
Vertical
Precise
In relief
Angular or semi-angular
T-bars and f-bars strong and prolonged
Signature placed to the right
Signature underlined
Lines horizontal and parallel
Left margin regular

Ex. 23. - Will power, but with impulsiveness

Veuillez agréer, cher Monsieur, avec mes remerciements, nos compliments et mes hommages pour Madame Delamain. et pour vous l'assurance de mes sentiments tout dévoués -

Ch. Jacquiot.

Ex. 24. - Will power, but with self-control

THE FOUR PRINCIPAL PSYCHIC
FUNCTIONS AND THE
TYPES DERIVING FROM THEM

In order to adapt to the outside world and to the conditions of his own disposition, the individual has at his command, four principal functions, which are: *Thinking, Feeling, Sensation* and *Intuition.*

The will, as we have seen, should not be considered as a psychic function, but as the sum of the energy capable of animating the functions.

The *principal psychic functions* are inborn elements arising from the core of the psyche.

We can define a function as a psychic activity that, in different conditions and circumstances, retains its own character and acts in a predetermined fashion, independently of its contents. Therefore, it is not important, when evaluating the predominance of *Thinking* for example, to consider *what the individual thinks* when faced with this or that situation. What is important is that he confronts that situation *with the help* of Thinking and not Feeling or another function. Of the four functions it is the one that customarily prevails in a person that will characterise his type.

Jung's two typologies (extraverted and introverted, attitudes and functions) are founded on the conception of an unconscious; that is to say, of a part of the psyche unknown to the individual, but nevertheless active and effective. The four functions just mentioned, act partly in the unconscious, but these functions are more subtly shaded and productive in the individual when they are more conscious; in other words, when they are accessible and usable to him.

The four principal functions act in the following way :

Sensation ascertains what exists around us; it is pure perception. It is also called "the reality function".

Thinking indicates to us the meaning of things perceived.

Feeling transmits to us the value that this thing has for us. It establishes the relationship between the subject and object, which it accepts or refuses.

Intuition reveals the possibilities inherent in a thing, a person or a situation. It is the function of spontaneous, unreflective comprehension, arrived at through the unconscious.

Thanks to these four functions, the individual's orientation in the world is just as complete as geographical orientation is by longitude and latitude. "The four functions are similar to the four cardinal points and are as arbitrary and indispensable as the latter".

It is often asked of Dr. Jung why he reduced the number of psychic functions to four. This number, quite simply, is the result of his experience. It corresponds to the necessity for psychic equilibrium. The old concept of the four temperaments corresponded to the same need for equilibrium and harmony.

Every human being has these four functions, in different degrees of development. One of them is generally more developed and more conscious than the other three and will be the *principal function*. A second serves as an auxiliary (or adjoining) function. The third and fourth are more or less unconscious and rudimentary.

This distribution of the functions is the most common, but there are cases in which one predominates to the point of stifling the other three. There exist also some not very highly evolved beings in whom no function prevails, for they are all more or less unconscious.

A great number of the psychic disorders from which humanity suffers, come from the uneven development of these four functions, which are our means of adapting to the world. If all of them are developed to the same degree or each one clearly distinguished from the others, and thereby suited for the work proper to it, these disorders would be less frequent, but they often originate from the exaggerated development of the principal function to the detriment of the others. The predominant function is, so to speak, "insatiable". The Thinking type would want only to think; the Feeling type desires only to feel. Deprived of their full conscious value, the inferior functions become pro-portionately more and more unconscious as the libido is withdrawn from them, to be added to the principal, already overloaded function.

However, each function, each instinct preserves a part of the energy that is proper to it. When the inferior functions are set aside too much, they fall into the unconscious, to a primitive level. They are then in opposition to the intentions of the conscious and become detrimental, for *the libido is always dynamic : it creates or it destroys.*

The *principal function* decides the functional type. We therefore have the *Thinking type*, the scholar, for example, the *Feeling type*, certain poets, the *Sensation type*, the practical and resourceful man, and the *Intuitive type*, the inventor and the mystic.

The man who, being objective and logical, confronts a situation with his reason while instinctively setting aside the feeling that could, by its subjective judgements, disturb his objective thinking, represents the *Thinking type*.

The man (or, more often, the woman) who principally uses his refined feeling, tending to be in direct contact with the object, saying : I love or do not love this, represents the *Feeling type*. Thinking, as a function opposed to Feeling, is at the opposite pole to this psychological type.

The man who keenly perceives everything communicated by the senses - smell, touch, sight, hearing and who is very conscious of all physical manifestations, but weak in intuition (the opposite function), represents the *Sensation type*.

Lastly, he (or often she) who perceives the totality of a given thing, even when complicated, in an immediate, exact way, but is weak and often deficient with regard to the practical exigencies of life, represents the *Intuition type*.

Thinking is the function that arranges ideas into a logical whole. It is an activity of apperception, which may be active or passive. Active thinking represents an act of the will. Passive thinking, on the contrary, does not obey our will; it is something to which we submit. The simple linking of ideas, called by certain psychologists (James) associative thinking, is not active thinking, but merely representation. One should speak of thinking only when there is a union of ideas by comprehension, where there is an act of judgement. Jung calls the capacity for directed thinking, intellect, and the capacity for passive or non-directed thinking, intellectual intuition. He says that sentimental thinking is not intuitive thinking, but a kind of thinking that depends on feeling, that is to say, a thinking that follows no logical principle, but is subject to the principle of feeling. In sentimental thinking, the laws of logic are suppressed in favour of sentimental purpose.

Feeling represents an independent function, a function of the heart (*Gemüt*). It is something that takes place between

the Ego and a object of whatever kind, an act in which the
Ego attributes a certain value to this object, in the sense of
its being desirable or undesirable (*Lust and Unlust*). Feeling
is an absolutely subjective function, which can be
independent of an impression coming from the outside, but
which can also be associated with a sensation. Feeling, when
it is exalted in its intensity, gives rise to what is called an
affective state.

Intellectual concepts are incapable of adequately
describing feeling, for thinking belongs to another domain.
Already, the idea of classifying the functions is an
intellectual exercise and therefore incompatible with the
essence of feeling. In the face of such an impossible situation,
one has to be content with the limitations of intellectual
concepts for describing feeling.

Feeling is comparable to intellectual apperception in so
far as it is the recognition of a value. It can be expressed
actively or passively. It is passive in nature when a state of
things, of whatever kind, evokes it and attracts it, but is
active when it intentionally puts a value on stimuli coming
from the outside, when it makes a choice. This activity is of a
truly sentimental and not an intellectual kind. Active feeling
is therefore a directed function, an act of will : for example,
"to love," in contrast to "to be loving." The latter would
indicate passive feeling not consciously directed. Language
expresses it by defining *to love* as an action, *to be loving* as a
condition.

Intuition is a flair, a conception of inherent possibilities in
a person, a situation or a thing. Intuition is the psychological
function that communicates perceptions to us by way of the
unconscious. Events from the outer or inner world, or their
invisible links, can be the object of this immediate
perception. "For intuition, a notion of whatever kind
presents itself as a totality, from the outset, without our
being able to discover or distinguish how it has presented

itself to us. Intuition is a kind of instinctive conception.... These notions, as in Sensation, have an *a priori* character, in contrast to the deductive or productive character of the judgements of Feeling or Thinking. Thus, intuitive conceptions have the character of certitude and infallibility that prompted Spinoza to consider Intuition as the supreme form of knowledge".

Sensation is the function of perception. We should clearly distinguish Sensation from Feeling, for the latter represents an entirely different *processus*. It may, however, be associated with Sensation by giving it an affective tone. Sensation is not only related to the physical excitation coming from the outside, but also, in the case of introversion, to all excitations coming from the inside : for example, from our organic state. Therefore, Sensation is first of all, perception by way of the senses... It strongly characterises the nature of the child and of primitive man... This function is a basic phenomenon not subject to the laws of reason, contrary to our notions of what constitutes thinking and feeling.

Paul Eluard makes a veritable declaration of faith in the senses when he says: "I do not believe in reconciling myself to the world through power of the intellect alone; I want everything to be responsive, real, useful to me, for it is only from this standpoint that I understand my existence." (To Pablo Picasso). See P. Eluard's handwriting, Ex. 31, p.104.

Sensation and Intuition are both non-rational functions of perception. Intuition is in a compensatory relation to Sensation. With the latter, it is the mother earth where the rational functions of Thinking and Feeling are born.

Jung's bi-partition of the functions has often been criticised, especially his categorising of Feeling as a "rational" function. But, is it not the common character of Thinking and Feeling to produce judgments : "This is true" and "This is pleasing?".

Perhaps, one could call them "judicial functions". But, Jung's terminology is accepted. Moreover, doesn't Pascal say: "The heart has its reasons that reason does not know?"

Jung considers the Thinking and Feeling functions as rational because they are based on a scale of values (objective or subjective) and the Sensation and Intuition functions as irrational because they perceive or "detect" things without the intervention of judgement.

Now, let us observe *how the functions interact with each other*. A rational function may have as auxiliary a non-rational function : for example, Thinking is often animated by Intuition. A non-rational function is helped by a rational function; Sensation, for example, is assisted by Feeling or Thinking: but neither the two rational functions nor the two non-rational functions are of help to each other. It is impossible to feel (a subjective activity, by definition) and to think (an objective activity) at the same time. Neither can one clearly perceive practical realities and, simultaneously, follow intuitive inspirations.

The two typologies just sketched out complement and interpenetrate each other. *Each function can be either extraverted or introverted*. There are as a result *eight variants. The extraverted or introverted thinker : the feeling type who exteriorises or hides his feelings : the sensation type who dominates the practical world* or who *leads the life of an aesthete withdrawn from the world* : the *extraverted intuitive type* who pursues the possibilities in his domain: (art, fashion, politics, commerce): or *the introverted type* (the mystics, some psychologists and great thinkers).

The *extraverted Thinking* type proceeds essentially by means of logical deduction, orientating himself toward objective criteria. He is an empirical thinker. His thinking is impersonal and constructive. He learns and assimilates easily, using current methods of deduction. He quickly finds the role that suits him : scholar, statesman, financier, lawyer, journalist, priest, teacher, architect, engineer, etc.

He adapts to all situations demanding a constructive talent that is orientated towards objective life. But the inflexibility of his judgments is such that this type, when pushed to the extreme, often becomes intolerant, fanatical, even tyrannical or, to a lesser degree, a tyrant in the home. His feeling is severely curbed, often repressed : hence his lack of sympathy for others, unless they share his ideas. The unconscious, with its compensatory and supplementary function, then reacts in the form of a childish sentimentality and an exaggerated self-esteem.

The *introverted Thinking* type prefers pure speculation to the realisation of his ideas. What is important to him, above all else, is the play of the mind. In this he will display a remarkable logic. If intuition enters into this combination, it creates the sudden insights of the true philosopher: but it is the system, the method, in the world of ideas, that, for the introverted thinker, will be the most essential. In contrast to the extraverted thinker, who organises ideas already in existence, the introverted thinker is interested only in the production of new ideas, or in combinations of ideas, often subtly shaded with mysticism, that give rise to images springing from his unconscious. As Jung says: "The facts are reassembled as proofs or as examples of a theory, but never for their own interest." The introverted thinker has a tendency to be dogmatic and intransigent in his opinions, which he imposes on others if he can be bothered with people at all. Sometimes he likes to surround himself with young people, who serve as an audience.

By nature the *extraverted Feeling* types are always on good terms with their intimate circle. When a well developed Sensation function is auxiliary to this principal function, we find ourselves face to face with a sympathetic, open, friendly person, ready to welcome one and all : the postman on the street, the vicar, or the neighbour's cat.

The extraverted Feeling type animates everything that he touches; by his communicative warmth he knows how to win hearts, hence his popularity. Never misled or overcome by his feelings, unlike the thinker to whom feeling isn't very familiar, he understands the world and knows how to evaluate people's character. On arriving in a new place, he gets to know the whole village within a few days, or the whole district with amazing ease. His numerous friends are very attached to him. Only the occasional judgement, harsh or lacking in tact, can be hurtful : an awkward remnant of destructive thinking, because it is insufficiently controlled. He says what he thinks, even bluntly, not afraid, like the introvert, of breaking a relationship, since he is always sure of being able to re-establish it.

Like all extraverts, this type also has his introverted side. In this type of nature largely directed toward the outside world, introversion takes the form of musing about the self. A veritable panic hits them when faced with solitude, a flight from the inner world. Their dreams are often peopled with frightening monsters, emanations from a poorly understood unconscious, with its unleashed energies. They are haunted by nightmares, which they may recount in the morning, without, however wanting to understand their meaning.

In extreme cases, Feeling, when perpetually exteriorised, tends to become affected and false. It mills around in a void.

The Feeling type is bound to the world by a network of diverse attachments, living in an abundance of projections of all kinds. For example, certain Feeling-type women project their Thinking, childish and incapable of abstraction, onto a man of the Thinking type, who becomes thereby "the most intelligent person in the world." This projection absolves them, in an agreeable manner, from thinking for themselves.

Others may on the other hand, manifest an unfortunate love for Thinking. They then split hairs in a personal philosophy that is entirely subjective, which their companion bears with amusement, irritation, or disdainful pity.

Women of the Feeling type, infinitely happy in a union for life, are, by the same token, very unhappy when that union miscarries or succumbs to the blows of destiny. Living for their social contacts , they are, of all human beings, those who most depend on others. The Thinking type can always take refuge in his ideological speculations: the Sensation type becomes tipsy with what he calls real pleasures : the Intuitive conceives of new possibilities in the most hopeless situations, and his imagination replenishes any void whatever. The Feeling type is like a fish out of water when the chief relationship of his life breaks up. It is only in a new union that he can recover his balance.

However, to be open to feeling, it is important that other functions do not intervene to upset Feeling, and nothing upsets it so much as thinking. The Feeling woman, therefore, represses thinking, as much as possible which she will only acknowledge as a servant, or better still as a slave of Feeling, but, as one cannot completely destroy logic and its deductions, they survive in the unconscious. Thus, repressed, thinking assumes bizarre or fantastic shapes : it becomes infantile, archaic and negative : it slips in between the individual and the love-object, to disparage and demolish it.

While the extraverted Feeling type is easy enough to fathom, this is not so with the *introverted Feeling* type, which is most common among women.

Under an apparently tranquil appearance, these women hide violent passions. They are tenacious and faithful. The same ardour that spontaneously drives an extraverted Feeling type toward a new object, ties the introverted Feeling type to one person.

Occasionally, the strength of feeling which they cannot exteriorise, is suddenly manifested in a gesture of sacrifice or heroism. However, their tense and passionate characters can also drive them to acts of cruelty and vengeance, for example: the harsh stepmother, who loves her own child and is cruel to her stepchild.

Extraverted Feeling gives the character grace, charm and an extraordinary radiance. Introverted Feeling, on the contrary, through its accumulated intensity, alienates, often creating a tragic atmosphere.

The *extraverted Sensation* type has a remarkably well developed sense of reality. He aspires to the enjoyment of concrete things : the manifestations of the inner life seem to him useless and unhealthy. He reduces everything to objective causes, to influences coming from the outside. If he is in a bad humour, or if he has a migraine, it is the bad weather that causes it. In his amorous relationships, the extraverted Sensation type will always allow himself to be guided by beauty, by physical charms. His ideal is called: Reality.

Those known as *bons vivants* (Sanguine temperament) belong to this class: gastronomes, restaurateurs, as well as manufacturers or merchants skilled in business; also engineers and skilled mechanics. With a well developed auxiliary Thinking function, they know how to master practical realities. On the other hand, their inferior function, Intuition, is under-developed and works in their unconscious resulting in absurd ideas, dramatics, superstitions and feelings without a reasonable basis, which distort the reality so much admired by them.

This reaction of deficient Intuition affects both extra-verted and introverted Sensation types.

The *introverted Sensation* type is well understood. A woman of this type is often imbued with an aura of mystery. The Sensation introvert is, above all, preoccupied with his own person and feels the slightest reactions in his organism with a surprising intensity and exactness. His attitude towards persons and things is often hesitant and mistrustful. He automatically rejects any situations where, unconsciously he feels concerned, like those children who always say "no" even before knowing what the matter is about. Endowed with extreme sensitivity and susceptibility, he feels every criticism as if it were a wound. To the same group belong those aesthetic natures who with extraordinary refinement savour a tone, a colour, a perfume, or, who can experience an amorous adventure in all its sensuous nuances without putting into it a true feeling of love or affection. Huysmans paints this kind of character and Oscar Wilde, a Sensation type par excellence, brought to life another example of it in his *Picture of Dorian Gray*.

The *extraverted Intuition* type is constantly in search of possibilities. He takes in at a glance all the eventualities of a situation. It is the unknown, the novelty, that attracts him. Relying on the past, he orientates himself toward the future more than being preoccupied with the reality of the moment. He always lives in anticipation. This character trait is often found in explorers and inventors. Attracted to a new idea, they abandon their work without waiting to gather its fruits. By the time others become aware of an interest in their invention or discovery, they have already discarded it, in pursuit of new projects.

A woman of this type will seek new relationships, interesting encounters and all the advantages that society can offer her. With Feeling as the auxiliary function, she will, with her flair, benefit those whom she loves. Have we not seen many a woman who has pushed her husband into an advantageous career that by himself, he would never have discovered?

The *introverted Intuition* type is no more interested than the extravert in the realisation of his ideas, which are often visionary and inspirational. To him, reality is his unconscious, peopled with images, his inexhaustibly rich inner world. The figures like the prophet Daniel, Cassandra, poets like Gérard de Nerval and certain great mystics, illustrate this group rather well.

For the intuitive introvert, the Sensation function is often deficient. Absorbed in his inner life, he lacks adequate perception of outside realities, all the more so because his observational sense is often wanting. He lacks vital contact with tangible reality : he forgets or neglects his own person. This human type is easily misunderstood and under-estimated, and it is only with deeper understanding that one starts to render him justice.

One should repeat that this typology does not represent a scale of values. Each type has its own characteristics and importance in the totality of life, its possibilities and its dangers.

When we find ourselves in the presence of a rather marked personality type, it is easy to tie him to his attitude and functional type. But, in many cases, the problem is more complex, for it is important to understand that many people do not live according to their best function. Disregarding their true nature, they rely on a less developed function, and sometimes, even, on their deficient function.

It is obvious that the ideal state would be one of perfect balance between the four functions : but the person in possession of equally developed Thinking, Intuition, Sensation and Feeling functions, is, for all practical purpose never encountered. On the other hand, each one of us can progressively develop our less differentiated functions by consciously turning towards them, which is a first step towards improving them.

As we have seen, every person has the four functions, which develop partly in the unconscious, unless they are not properly differentiated. In the latter case, the individual reacts by Thinking at a time when it would be useful to use Feeling, and vice versa, whence, discordancies in character and behaviour.

Once again it should be understood that the development of an inferior function passes first of all though the adjoining function. A Thinking-Intuition type, desirous, for example, of opening up his Feeling, exerts an influence upon it by using his Intuition as the mediator.

A dual task is incumbent upon us : firstly, to render conscious and develop our deficient functions in order to find a necessary balance and realise our latent energies and, secondly, to develop to the maximum degree our principal function : the one we are master of, which will give us a sense of fulfilment.

The play of the functions takes place not only at the core of the individual, but also in his *relationships with others*. One frequently sees that marriages, friendships and even partnerships are mainly entered into from the angle of an eventual compensation. Thus, the extravert more or less unconsciously seeks out the introvert, the Thinking type is attracted by the Feeling type, and vice versa. We can say, in principle, that "extremes touch each other" and that "opposites attract each other".

But, what a tragedy, or often, what a comedy, it can be when these opposite types, always in search of each other, do not achieve an understanding of one another. Each one reproaches in his partner exactly those virtues or weaknesses that caused him to make such a choice. The extravert finds the introvert too dry, too disdainful, cold, unsociable. The introvert, for his part, judges the former to be superficial, frivolous and needlessly busy.

Experience has shown us that unions between types of the same group evolve in the following classic fashion: for example, take a couple, both introverts. There is at first understanding, because of the similarity. The spouses are not sociable, they isolate themselves from the world and break off contact with others. They are happy in their solitude, but soon an atmosphere of coldness pervades their home, a lack of warmth and charm, which can also stifle children forced to live in this environment. At the slightest matrimonial difficulty, the two spouses will move further and further away from each other, without knowing how to build a bridge, as each one remains in his shell. A silence grows, filled with repressed reproaches, with unexpressed grievances that can become unscaleable mountains. A storm would be much healthier than this accumulation of electricity that is never discharged, or which, only after years, will, explode into an eruption so violent that it will destroy the marriage.

Thus couples, apparently united and apparently in harmony sometimes end up by separating or divorcing, without there ever having been on either side, an outside amorous attraction, or reason of any other kind. The marriage is undone quite simply because the two partners have never exteriorised their feelings.

Let us take another extreme case: marriage between two extraverts. The household of such a couple resembles a railway station more than a home. There is no rest in it, one is never alone. From morning till night, a thousand fashionable or social events are always in progress: visits from friends, dinners, going out. They live in a state of restlessness, of general distraction: and, despite the warmth of the atmosphere, one senses an emptiness beneath all this hustle and bustle. There is no chance for intellectual or artistic accomplishment under such conditions.

As a result the extraverted man allows himself to be attracted by an introverted woman whose calmness and strength of feeling are for him an island of repose on which he can at last rest his weary soul. The wife, for her part, will be attracted by someone who represents a centre of interest and depth of soul that, until then, she had not found in herself or her husband. This family drama, may astonish everyone in the family circle, but is nevertheless, psychologically inevitable.

Unions between types of opposite groups are so frequent that one may observe them every day. These marriages or partnerships correspond to a vital need. Looking at them more closely, one notices that the selection is made not only according to the complementary attitude, but also *according to the functions*.

The Thinking type needs Feeling, the Intuitive needs Sensation and vice versa. It is a matter for conjecture to what degree the individual unconsciously complements his deficient functions. The best households are those in which the marriage partners find in each other a function which they share. For example, the husband who is a Thinking type with Sensation as an auxiliary function, and a wife who is a Feeling type also with Sensation as a secondary function, will understand each other marvellously in the sensual area, in the broadest sense of this word. They will both like good food, all the pleasures that a life of the senses offers. They can go further and find a mutual taste for luxury or for art objects. There will always be an area in which an easy and spontaneous understanding will occur. This area of agreement will be their refuge when there are difficulties of an intellectual or sentimental kind.

When two people of an entirely different type meet, say for example, an Intuitive woman and a Sensation-type man, an irresistible attraction may occur, but it does not necessarily imply harmony.

The two partners evolve on levels that are too disparate for them to be able to understand each other.

Another characteristic case: an extraverted woman marries an introverted man. If the man dominates the woman by the force of his personality, she is obliged to follow him into his isolation, or, on the other hand in order to render this union viable and to compensate for her husband's deficiencies, she may be forced into an excessive extraversion that finally exhausts her. Unwittingly, a person of an extreme type can encumber the partner with all the obligations of the outer life, or, for that matter, the inner life, for, not only does the soul aspire to an equilibrium, but so do the couple. One of the partners can drive the other into a state of conflict, or even into a neurosis, quite simply because of an unwillingness to pay the price of adapting to the other's attitude.

These illustrations which are very close to life, are of primary interest for graphologists, who are often asked for advice on the subject of eventual marriages.

Let us quote here one of Jung's passing remarks on his typology: In a union of whatever sort, there is always one partner who "controls the other," and one partner who "is controlled". That is to say, there is always one person stronger or more generous, who protects, or soothes the other, so to speak, who assumes the responsibilities, who plays the maternal or paternal role. This role is independent of age. The younger of the partners can adopt the role of the one who controls, but, it is noticeable that whenever a separation occurs, it is always the one who "controls" who breaks the union.

The Psychological Types at Dinner

In order truly to understand the different psychological types, their characteristic reactions and relationships, I should like to present them in a living situation.

The reader will then see the foregoing theories captured in the flesh, and get to know all these people, men and women, whose character-types have been sketched out. Let us therefore imagine a dinner party at which all of them are brought together.

Naturally, it is the *Feeling type* who receives. She is a charming woman, well built, very feminine, such as Renoir liked to paint; Dr. Corman's expansive type; the Venus type in the old classification. Extraverted, very sociable, a cyclothyme, according to Dr. Kretschmer, she is the perfect lady of the house. Pretty, friendly, skilful, she creates around her an atmosphere of benevolence and pleasant warmth.

Her conversation isn't especially interesting; she often repeats the opinions of her husband, her father, the parish priest, or the radio, adding nothing to them but her personal emotions. A curious thing: her judgements, her criticisms are often harsh, unjust and destructive, because Thinking, which is her inferior function, plays nasty tricks on her.

Her house is arranged with refined taste and her cuisine is excellent, for her husband is a gourmet and aesthete, and demands discreet luxury. He is an *introverted Sensation* type, an expert on old paintings and a collector of art objects. As his *auxiliary function* is *Thinking*, he has a splendid library. His favourite authors are Huysmans and Oscar Wilde, for he discovers something of himself in their works.

He is as taciturn as his wife is talkative. This party displeases him; he doesn't understand why all these uninteresting people have been invited, who draw him away from the delicious solitude of his study. But he allows his wife to organise their social life, for he knows from experience that she excels in the art of hospitality. She supplies him with the extraversion and openness to the outside world which he lacks.

He receives his guests with a somewhat cool and distant air and shakes the hand of the fashionable lawyer (belonging to the *extraverted Thinking* type, which he disdains), saying "goodbye" instead of saying "good evening"; a faux pas which his wife tries to make up for with redoubled kindness.

The *lawyer* has arrived first. He is well adjusted, has passed his examinations in brilliant fashion and is embarking upon a political career with a future. Although young, he has acquired a certain celebrity as a speaker, his judgment is clear, his logic perfect. He knows how to sway the public by the force of his arguments, which are always based on facts. *Sensation* being his *auxiliary function*, he is not much interested in abstract thought, has sound practical sense and good organisational abilities. His judgements are based essentially *on factors coming from the outside*, that is to say, on values transmitted to him *by tradition, the environment, education. The extraverted intellectual type* is, in fact, guided by objective factors.

This kind of thinking is the most generally recognised and accepted as belonging to the *Thinking* function. It differs a great deal from *introverted Thinking*, which is much more concerned with subjective factors, giving rise to independent theories and judgments built on subjective experiences.

Then the businessman, *the industrialist*, arrives with his wife. He belongs to the *extraverted Sensation type*, she to the *introverted Feeling type*. Here we see how opposites attract and complement each other.

The industrialist has good sense, is active, busy, practical and resourceful. He directs a veritable army of employees with authority and intelligence. His days are filled with diverse pursuits, commercial and social.

Let us note, however, that he often seems to lack foresight: in him *Intuition*, the function opposite to Sensation, is poorly developed. He understands things only when they have become palpable realities.

No one understands the tie which binds this couple. The husband is well dressed, but a bit crude: he lacks finesse and delicacy. He is noisy, he talks too much and drinks a good deal. He is a heavy eater : Dr. Corman's *expansive type*.

His wife, on the other hand, is silent and enigmatic. She is like still, deep waters, but - a fact that interests the lady of the house, the specialist in human relations - is the surprising *influence* that this young woman of insignificant appearance exerts over her husband. She has completely subdued him and he follows her with his eyes whenever she moves away. He asks her advice on every issue.

There is no mystery here for the psychologist who knows the law of opposites: for this man (Sensation-Thinking type), his wife represents the *Feeling* and *Intuition* weakly developed in himself. It is she who symbolises and incarnates the soul, the inner life, which for him has remained absolutely unconscious. He projects his soul onto her.

The *introverted Feeling type*, frequently women, but sometimes also found in men, particularly artists and musicians, do not exteriorise their emotions. They accumulate and interiorise them, and this mass of libido creates an atmosphere which is strongly attractive because of its mysterious quality. The Feeling type in question, the industrialist's wife, has a great passion for music which is the purest expression of her feelings. It is in the world of harmonies that she exteriorises, more than in life : it is there that she is happy.

Next arrives the *introverted Thinker*. He is a doctor, a specialist in sleeping sickness. He doesn't practise medicine, for patients don't interest him. Passionately fond of scientific research, he brings to this field his particular ideas and personal theories.

One never sees his wife: he doesn't go out with her. It is whispered that she is quite uncultured, a simple woman who was formerly his cook. Here again, the opposites attract : this good woman belongs to the *extraverted Feeling type*. The scientist has married his inferior function, which happens rather frequently.

Finally, the last guest enters in haste, an aeronautical engineer. Breathless, he talks about his latest invention, a new aeroplane of entirely novel conception. He is an *extraverted Intuitive type*, bubbling over with new ideas. But, as his sense of reality is deficient, he never achieves his dreams. He talks about travelling and future projects. At last, seated at the table, he bolts down the excellent food, without even noticing what he is eating.

The conversation becomes animated. Politics, theatre, lawsuits, the cinema are discussed. The exraverted Thinking and Sensation types, the lawyer and the industrialist, keep the conversational ball rolling. The introverted Thinker keeps quiet, being awkward, like many of his kind, and feeling ill at ease in this worldly environment.

Finally, toward the end of the dinner, having warmed up a bit, he comes out of his shell.

He talks about his theory on sleeping sickness, but, as his Feeling function is not very well developed, he doesn't realise the reaction that such a subject evokes among the guests and blunders on - as people who are poorly adjusted to the world often do.

At this evening party the men around the table, listen to him with a certain interest. The extraverted Thinking type follows the introverted Thinker, because everything in the world of ideas interests him. The extraverted Sensation type thinks about the practical application of studies on sleeping sickness.

The introverted Sensation type, the aesthete, is quite simply disgusted by a subject of conversation that troubles his digestion, but, the most irritated is his wife, the lady of the house.

At the beginning of this long discourse, she had tried in vain to change the course of the conversation. Now, tired, she loses the thread of it. Theoretical thought, devoid of all human feeling, eludes her and she feels it to be almost an insult. Her face, until now radiant, becomes dull. She is mortally bored. She comes to life again when they get up from the table. Quickly, she leads the industrialist's wife into the children's room, where in the warmth of their maternal roles, they can communicate.

One place at the table has remained vacant. It is that of the poet, the *introverted Intuitive type*. He didn't come, he didn't even telephone to apologise. He had forgotten the invitation.

This is how he passed his evening: absorbed in his manuscript right until evening, he dragged himself away to the little corner restaurant where he ate frugally, for he is poor. He is basically a retiring type of person, tall, thin, with a slender, elongated face.

He got to the restaurant very late; as he lives outside time and space, he had already lost half an hour looking for his spectacles before leaving. But, it was of little importance to him that he ate so meagrely. He glanced from time to time at the *Divine Comedy*, which he had brought with him.

Then he walked along the Seine, beneath the starry sky. He caught cold, for he had forgotten to bring his overcoat, not having realised that the weather changes with the start of winter.

Strolling along, he composed a metaphysical sonnet and was happy.

Suddenly, he remembered that he had been invited to dinner, but by now it was too late. The *forgetfulness* is a *flawed action*, which expresses very well the introvert's apprehension at going out into the world, his extreme timidity.

"Never mind! I'll send my verses to the lady of the house," he thought, "she'll have the best of me."

Maybe he will realise his intention, but will the Feeling type be able to appreciate this present?

And yet, this ill-clad Intuitive (for introverts often neglect themselves) this poor, somewhat ridiculous poet, with his vague and myopic eye, who flees human warmth, the joys and sorrows of others, has perhaps conceived an immortal poem that will make up for everything he has missed!

Who hasn't encountered these psychological types that I have just presented in depth? We all come close, more or less, to one of them.

And, all these types have a handwriting just as individual as they are themselves.

Through the specimens which follow, penned by several well known and representative writers, psychoanalysts will be able to realise, for their part, *what graphology can bring to psychoanalysis* : an immediate, quick and profound view of the whole. The scriptural gesture reveals, unquestionably, the individual's intellectual and cultural level, his vital energy, his character, his reactions in social life and his ultimate efficiency.

What the analyst learns about his subject by observing him for weeks and months, the graphologist can sum up in a single study. Many psychoanalysts benefit greatly by using this means of investigation.

As already mentioned, the *combination of the functions and attitudes produces eight variants* : extra - or introverted Thinking, extra - or introverted Feeling, extra - or introverted Sensation, extra - or introverted Intuition.

It will now suffice to list the graphic characteristics of each function: that is to say, the graphic signs of Thinking, Feeling, etc.: the signs of Thinking joined with those of extraversion already given, will yield the graphic signs of extraverted Thinking, and so on, for the other functions.

Graphic Expression of the Functions

Graphic expression of Thinking

Sober and simplified
Small, fine
Aerated, well spaced
Combined
Connected
Small and rounded
Orderly
Progressive
Sharp-pointed finals
Weak or short lower extensions
Typographical capitals
Signature simple, without ostentation

The above mentioned signs more or less unite to give the well known image of the writing of the scholar, the thinker. The handwritings [1] of the Thinking type ordinarily have a good general level.

---

(1) The samples shown can only be considered as "aspects", coming from more or less pure types. The reality, however is infinitely varied.

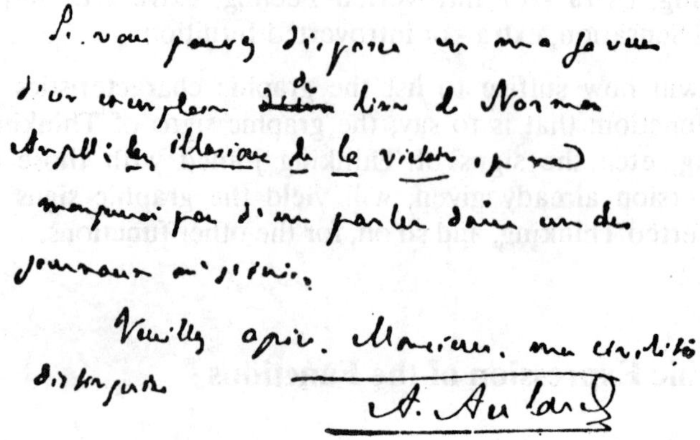

[handwritten letter in French, signature: A. Aulard]

Ex. 25. - Introverted Thinking, auxiliary function : Intuition.

Graphic expression of Feeling

Large
Spread out
Expanded
Garlands or angular garlands
Regular right slant
Finals in open curves
Slightly pasty, velvety pressure

In general, *the above-mentioned signs* should
    all be present, to reflect the Feeling function.

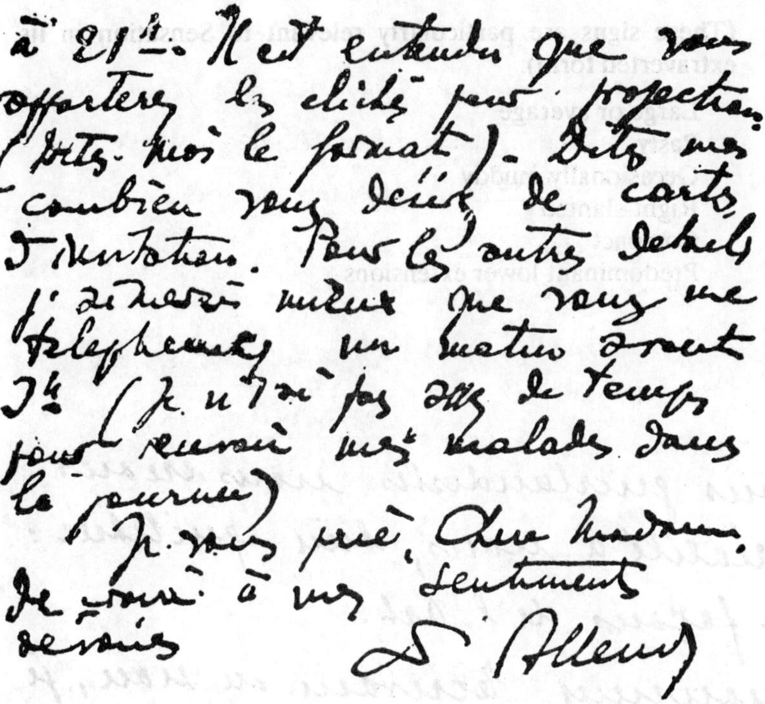
à 21h. Il est entendu que vous apporterez les clichés pour projection (dites-moi le format). Dites-moi combien vous désirez de cartes d'invitation. Pour les autres détails je désirerais mieux que vous me téléphoniez un matin avant 9h (je n'ai pas assez de temps pour recevoir mes malades dans la journée)
Je vous prie, Chère Madame, de croire à mes sentiments dévoués
Dr Allendy

Ex. 26. - Extraverted Thinking, auxiliary function: Sensation.

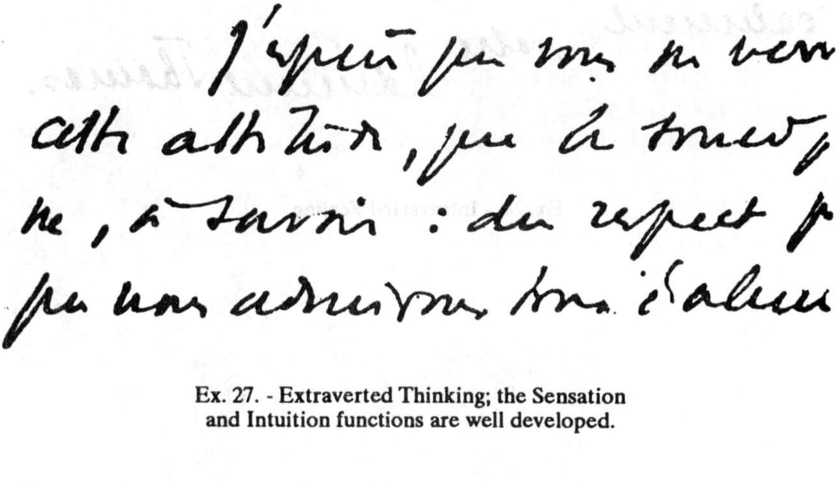
J'espère que vous ne verrez cette attitude, que la marque de, à savoir : du respect que nous admirons tous d'ailleurs

Ex. 27. - Extraverted Thinking; the Sensation and Intuition functions are well developed.

Graphic expression of Sensation

(These signs are particularly relevant to Sensation in its
extraverted form).

Large or average
Pasty
Occasionally muddy
Right-slanted
Compact
Predominant lower extensions

Ex. 28. - Introverted Feeling.

Sauf que je ne tiens
sur la traduction.
Je serais heureuse
qu'il sera possible
" mouvement Picasso".

Ex. 29. - Extraverted Feeling, auxiliary function: Sensation

Ex. 30. - Extraverted Feeling

The graphic expression of the Sensation function, in its introverted form, has another aspect, as follows:-

Ex. 31. - Paul Eluard's writing. Predominance of the Sensation function.

Ex. 32. - Colette's writing. Extraverted Sensation, auxiliary function: Feeling.

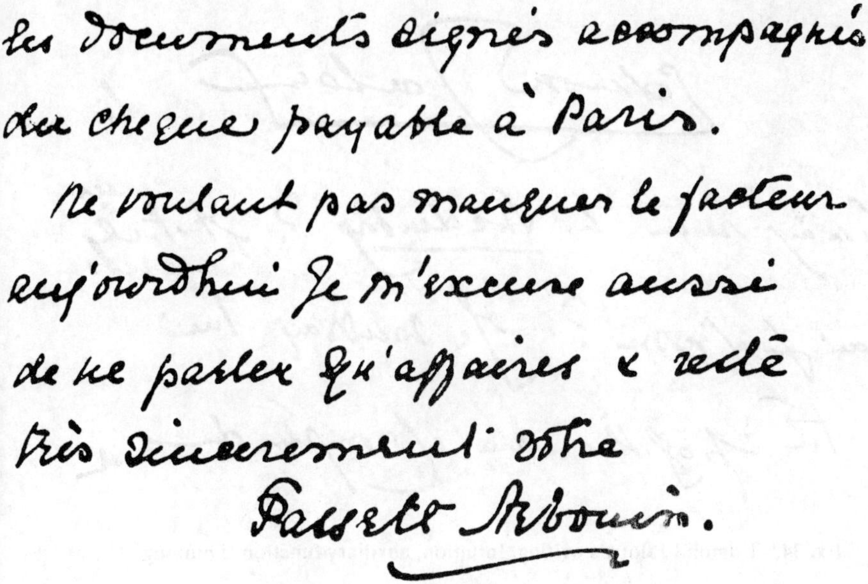

[handwritten text in French]

Ex. 33. - Introverted Sensation, auxiliary function : Thinking

Graphic expression of introverted Sensation

Slightly artificial, sometimes quite stylised (an artist's writing)
  Small, a bit complicated
  Slightly pasty pressure

Graphic expression of Intuition

  Light, thin
  An airy rhythm
  Disconnected or grouped
  Combined
  Ample and simplified
  Originality in the upper extensions
  Lower extensions in the form of a basin
  Irregular

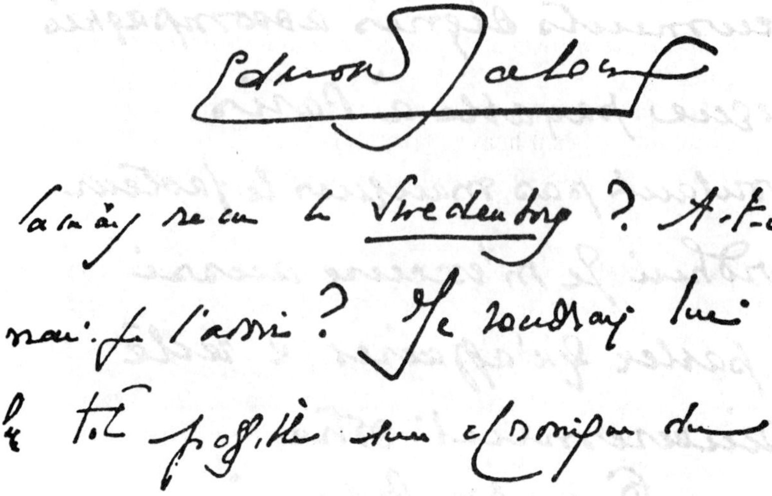

[Edmond Jaloux signature]

[handwritten text]

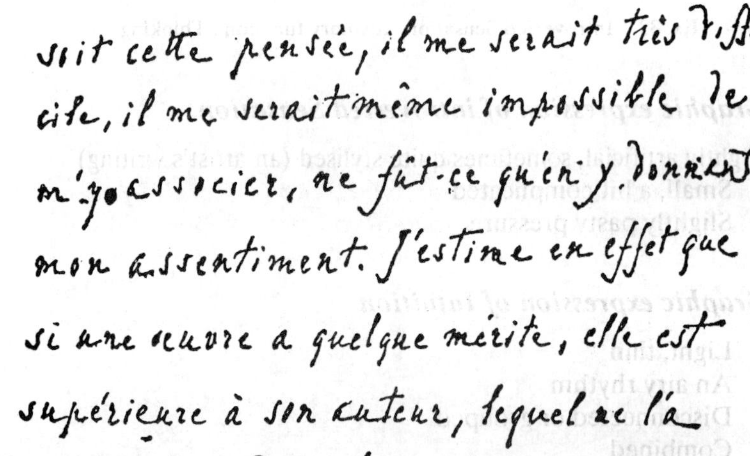

Ex. 34. - Edmond Jaloux's writing. Intuition, auxiliary function: Thinking.

[handwritten text]

Ex. 35. - Henri Bergson's writing. Intuition, auxiliary function: Thinking.

In general:

Thinking diminishes the size of the writing and concentrates it;

Feeling enlarges, expands and softens it;

Sensation makes it heavy and stabilises it;

Intuition lightens the writing, gives it movement, rhythm; and sometimes, instability.

The description of the psychic structures that I have just given does not pretend to encompass all the aspects of the character. No typology is limiting, and any other classification can combine with the one we offer to enrich it with fresh nuances. Every type of classification one comes across will be correct in itself and will take nothing from the correctness of the others.

The Four Temperaments and their Graphic Expression

Thus, the graphologist, after having determined the writer's attitude and function types, can very usefully try to discern the dominant element of his temperament by connecting it with the Bilious, Nervous, Sanguine or Lymphatic types. Below are some striking traits of these different types, according to Dr. Carton's work, *Diagnostic et Conduite des Temperaments* :

The Bilious subject is enterprising, the Nervous is agitated, the Sanguine gets carried away, the Lymphatic is calm.

In the *Bilious* subject, it is voluntary activity that dominates among his varied characteristics : tireless and incessant energy, authoritarianism, obstinacy, tenacity, a fighting spirit, resistance and combativeness.

Ex. 36. - Writing of the graphologist, Franzoni. Extraverted Intuition.

Ex. 37. - Halévy's writing. Intuition, Thinking.

The *Nervous* temperament relates to the domain of sensitivity and emotivity. Nervous subjects are generally hypersensitive, hyperimpressionable, agile, quick, suggestible, irregular and changeable. The *cerebral Nervous* type, who is cold in appearance, with a searching mind, curious, relective and comprehensive, can be distinguished from the *sensitive Nervous* type who is agitated, anxious, unstable and undisciplined.

Both are rather sombre, awkward in adapting, live on their nerves and are prone to negative and pessimistic attitudes, which are difficult for them to overcome. Mental activity is the foundation of their existence. Stimulation, pursuit of an ideal, searching for answers, the attraction of an interesting or pleasant occupation, are for them the best means of maintaining their interest in life.

The *Sanguine* temperament is broad and expansive. The Sanguine subject is vigorous, excitable, prone to exaggeration, imaginative, a traveller, optimistic, enthusiastic and jovial. He throws himself into things suddenly and on the spur of the moment and frequently unwisely; he waxes lyrical; he swells with anger and subsides just as quickly.

He is good at attack, poor at waiting. He hates being enclosed or restrained, he needs ample space, life in the open air, situations in which he can exert himself and shine. He is, in addition, kind, obliging, self-satisfied and imposing. His friendship is sincere and valuable : he is traditional, peaceful, generous and good-natured, but he lacks depth. His intelligence is lively, he is good at everything and is eloquent and adaptable, but his will is rather weak. His faults are intemperance, impatience, instability and vanity.

The *Lymphatic* subject is a more heavy, stolid sort. He has a calm character, nonchalant, placid, occasionally childish; in a word, passive. Slowness is the dominant element of this temperament.

me permet actuellement quelque
krais désireux – d'appartenir à v
toutefois elle recrute des membres, .

Ex. 38. - Bilious temperament.

Merci, cher
et bien cordi"

Ex. 39. - Sanguine temperament

à toute, La Bruyère donne bien ici une
ipales raisons de l' emploi de la politess
l' explique pas que suffisamment pour

Ex. 40. - Nervous temperament.

Voudriez vous me faire
l'année 1941, le coupon n° 3

Ex. 41. - Lymphatic temperament.

Gestures are rare, measured and slow. Speech is drawling and monotonous; conception is slow, approach to work, phlegmatic.

Sensitivity is attenuated, the imagination is cold, decisions are slow.

It the subject has superior mental qualities, this temperament gives him the virtues of composure, self-control, foresight, faithfulness, regularity, orderliness, sobriety and patience.

He applies the brake at the desired moment. If, on the other hand, the personality is weak, lymphatism leads to inaction, to letting things go, to a lack of cleanliness, to lack of foresight, to gluttony and laziness.

The Lymphatic subject is born to be commanded and goaded, for he often lacks initiative and activity. In daily life he avoids upsets, apathy, in this case, substituting for prudence.

The handwriting, of the *Bilious* is firm, regularly pressured on all the vertical strokes; that of the *Sanguine*, animated, or with superfluously crossed "t's" and pasty pressure.

The handwriting of the *Nervous* subject is irregular, jerky and thready.

The *Lymphatic* subject is characterised particularly by the monotony, regularity in size and direction and the softness and heaviness of the writing.

With the temperaments, as with the attitudes of extra-version or introversion, none exists in a pure state, but it is important to determine the one that predominates.

FORMATION OF THE CHARACTER

The graphologist who analyses a handwriting finds himself confronting an established character, made up of a certain cluster of traits which consistently appear together. For example, a writer may simultaneously appear to be stubborn, miserly, meticulous and animated by a spirit of domination. Too often, the graphologist notes this cluster of particular qualities without understanding the profound reasons behind their association. Why does one so often find avarice in conjunction with stubbornness, inveterate habit, order, and a spirit of domination? The graphologist should know why certain character traits are found together again and again. It is necessary, for that purpose, to study the formation of the character from earliest infancy.

Let us follow the path of the infant, resting securely it its mother's arms, on whom love and sustenance are lavished without question, right up to adulthood, when he must work hard to attain and achieve the necessities and amenities of life. This path consists of several stages, often strewn with obstacles and snares.

The first stage consists of the absorption and assimilation of nourishment and as the baby has no other concerns at this time, all pleasant sensations are centralised in these functions. It is a state of pure receptivity and passivity, of complete dependence on another person who gives without asking anything in return. The source from which this love and nurture come is the same. During this period, muscular activity in the small child is devoted to respiration and digestion. The "participation mystique" with the person who supplies these comforts, the mother or nurse, is absolute [1].

The end of this phase of complete bliss comes with *weaning*. Children who have been too abruptly or unlovingly weaned, retain throughout their life a vague and diffuse feeling of something missing, a deprivation, an unsatisfied avidity, a constant desire to possess, which never leaves them.

The greatest crisis, however, in the small child's development, occurs at the time of toilet training. It is important because, for the first time in his life, the child is no longer free to do just as he wishes. This obligation involves several different factors: 1. The child must master his muscular functioning, which presupposes a conscious act. 2. He must give something of himself (his excrement). 3. He must adjust to his environment: that is to say, must perform at a certain time or when it is asked of him. Thus, the attention which up to that point had been devoted solely to the absorption of nourishment and to the mouth, as the principal organ, must from then onwards also be turned towards the organs and products of elimination.

---

(1) The term "participation mystique" is borrowed from Lévy-Bruhl (*Les Fonctions mentales dans les Sociétés inférieurs*, Paris, 1912). It expresses the unconscious fusion of psyche, a partial identity between subject and object. The *participation mystique* was first observed among primitive tribes, wherein man becomes one with other men, with animals, with all of nature. Analytical psychology has been able to verify that this state of mind also exists in the unconscious of civilised men: it may be the vestige of a primitive state. See A. Teillard, *Le Symbolisme du Rêve*.

The child *thus goes from the oral (or buccal) phase*, to the *anal phase*. For the first time he enters into a social milieu in which he no longer only takes, but also gives and fulfils his duties.

The child very quickly realises the power he wields over his entourage: parents, nurse, brothers and sisters, who sometimes literally pay him court, who admire him and reward him for what he has "done", or scold and punish him for what he has done badly or not at all. One may observe entire families gathered around a baby on his "throne".

It is during this period that the outlines of the child's character are sharply drawn. Freud and Adler insist on the fact that the character is firmly established by the age of two or three years. At this age, the child understands that he possesses something of his own.

He understands, in addition, that love, concern, caresses, rewards are forthcoming when he gives, but that he also has the power either to annoy or to please those around him. He keeps for himself and holds back, or he relaxes and lets go. Feelings of possession, egoism, miserliness, stubbornness, obstinacy, power over others are thus shaped simultaneously. The passivity of the infant turns into activity, or even aggressivity, in the growing child. Complete union with the beloved person is transformed into a duality and gives way to a process of change. Absolute dependence is followed by a feeling of power over the love-object, whom the child, from then on, can satisfy or deprive. Aggressiveness may increase and reach the point of sadism: that is to say, pleasure in causing suffering.

All educators know the concern small children feel for their first products (excrement) and they know about children's games on this subject. Freud, to whom we owe these discoveries, deduces from these childish activities, man's tendencies to model in clay and dough.

Normally, after a latency period, the child enters the *genital stage* : he discovers his sexuality. Interest, up till now devoted to the anal zone, is transferred to the genital zone. But this transition does not always succeed. Often, the interest, instead of being dissociated from the oral and anal zones, remains fixed there, at least in part. Sexual perversions are formed at this time and the character, as well as the sexuality, fail to reach complete maturity. Freud relates male homosexuality to this regression, which is a complete or partial attachment to the anal zone. On the other hand, the *Mother Complex*, which we will look at further, also plays a large part in it.

What is important for the psychologist to know is the reverberation of this development on the character and how successfully it has been achieved. The individual who remains at one of the stages preliminary to adulthood, retains throughout life an infantile egoism and egocentricity.

The attainment of maturity presupposes the power to give, the power to love, to be ready to give of oneself, to make a creative effort. The individual attached to the oral or anal stage is a *narcissist*, in love with himself. This condition is justified in the small child, but implicit in it is the inability to live an adult life. The anal stage unfolds as a transition from egocentric and manipulative behaviour to sacrificial and altruistic behaviour. It is during this stage of development that the child must achieve this change in order to reach psychic fullness.

The sado-anal character, customary to one who has retained the egoism, aggressiveness, sadism, and avarice, characteristic of that stage, turns loving into a sort of blackmail, where he always manages to exploit the other. He doesn't want to give, only to receive.

One wouldn't need to be so concerned about this type of character, expect for the fact that it plays such an important role in social life.

Let us not forget the equation: Excrement = Gold = Money!

The useful donkey, who produces pieces of gold in fairy tales, produces them in a very natural way. Folklore sees gold in perspective as when someone one sets his left foot in excrement. In innumerable dreams, evacuations symbolise money.

The anal character accumulates treasures (avarice), dominates others and likes filth. Or else, he overcompensates his love of filth and ordure by an excessive care, order and propriety.

Here we confront the character of whom I spoke at the beginning of this chapter, who incorporates the group of tendencies: egoism, possessiveness, avarice, sense of order and spirit of domination.

Seeing, in different handwritings, these same characteristics so frequently combined, impelled me to seek their origin, which I found through psychoanalytical observation.

Pursuing our investigations further, even when transition from the anal stage to the genital stage proceeds normally, the healthy development of the adolescent is not yet assured. What will the adolescent do with his newly awakened sexual need? He can't satisfy it, especially in Western cultures, except in the form of auto-eroticism. Consequently, the majority of children will at this point come to the stage of masturbation.

Here, psychoanalysis takes a position other than that of the majority of parents and educators. We consider the onanism of puberty to be inevitable and harmless, provided the child's psyche is not poisoned by the fear and guilt-feelings that adults too often inculcate in him. In order to develop normally, the child should not be stimulated by overfeeding or the wrong sort of food. He should be pointed in the direction of sport and healthy games, thus lessening his need for masturbation. However, in principle, it is preferable that the child be interested in sex rather than risk a regression to the anal or oral stage. This regression is brought about too easily, when interest in the genital zone is thwarted by prohibition, threats and punishments.

The psychologist, whom many parents turn to when seeking advice, should place himself above moral prejudices. He must understand the libido or psychic energy is the same on whatever level or in whichever zone it is manifested. It is a question of whether the *vital principle* itself fully blooms allowing the capacity for love, confidence in oneself and in life, courage and particularly, creative energies to flower, or whether it fades away and dies.

Masturbation and adolescent homosexuality are less dangerous obstacles to the development of the child's personality than are, in the writer's opinion, under-handedness, hypocrisy and projection [1] of the unresolved complexes of the educator himself.

The adolescent stages are generally outgrown, but sometimes the complexes shaped in the course of childhood can only be resolved by means of analytical treatment.

Here are a few traits to be added to the picture of the oral and anal stages:

The oral stage is characterised by a naive, childish egoism and *avidity*. There is a predominance of the vegetative, life, interest being directed almost uniquely towards the absorption of food. Individuals who remain partly in this vegetative and passive state, retain the blissfulness of a baby. The cigar, or the pipe, often replace the baby's feeding bottle. When the infantile, passive attitude remains predominant, it produces characteristic neuroses: voracity, boulimia. At the slightest difficulty or sorrow in life, these

---

(1) See the following chapter.

people take refuge in their gluttony and as a consolation, eat far more than their systems require. (Another escape, not reserved for this type alone, is flight into sleep or illness).

Among the elderly, one often observes a *return to the oral stage*. Food will assume more and more importance for them and, during the restrictions of a war period, one can see grandparents vying with children for food.

Let us follow the evolution of the libido in the child [1].

Another *stage*, essential in the formation of the individual, begins when the child *becomes aware of its gender* and, by comparison, understands that it is a male or female.

When the little girl discovers that her brother or friend possesses "a thing she does not have" characteristic complexes arise, castration or mutilation complexes, which imply a serious general feeling of inferiority.

These complexes are either repressed, assimilated, or overcompensated. Often, the little girl copies the boy by adopting masculine attitudes. The desire of girls to be boys is well known.

Parents and teachers in their misunderstanding of the childish mind, frequently increase the little girl's feeling of inferiority, for example by saying to a boy, in her presence: "A boy doesn't do that," or "You are cowardly, like a girl," etc. Blunders of this kind produce traumatic shocks in children of both sexes.

In the little girl, the masculine complex, which Jung calls the *Animus*, and which is important for psychic balance, is found to be activated by utterances of this kind. It can hinder the development of the little girl in her femininity. Thus,

_____

(1) See : Dr. Françoise Marette, *Psychanalyse et Pédiatrie*. Charles Baudouin, *Indroduction à l'Analyse des Rêves*. Dr. René Allendy, *L'Enfance Méconnue*.

many pseudo intellectuals, who would be happier in their feminine role, choose a masculine profession in order to compensate for their inferiority complex. I have often observed this paradox in women undergoing psychoanalysis. As little girls they wanted to be equal to or surpass their brothers; as young women they act in opposition to their mother, whom they disapprove of because of their inferior state with regard to the father.

The young boy, when he discovers that, physically, the little girl possesses less than he does, may tend to depreciate women. Many homosexuals retain this attitude and make an exception only with regard to their own mother, or to women much older than they, whom they identify with their mother.

When he has reached the *genital stage* and has *become aware of his own sex*, around the age of eight, the child generally enters a *latency stage*, which lasts until approximately thirteen years of age. It is during this period that under normal conditions, the subject's relationship with the outside world is shaped and the intensity of love, until now directed toward his father or mother, brothers and sisters, emerges from the familial framework.

The difference between the masculine and feminine character, already apparent from infancy, becomes more and more evident. The little girl's character becomes more subjective and receptive, she wants to attract and please. The boy, more combative, is already off "to conquer the world".

After puberty, the interest of both sexes develops toward reciprocity, passing from the "I" towards the "You": that is to say, the adolescent finally turns away from the egocentric and auto-erotic stages to enter into the stage of falling in love; the creative stage, in the widest sense of the word.

Concern, until now concentrated on the subject of himself, turns towards the world of objects; towards the child, the fruit of love, the community, or the work of creation. The individual enters a state in which he gives more than he receives, instead of being only a recipient.

This, broadly outlined, is the normal evolution of character. We see to what degree instinct and feeling, body and soul interpenetrate each other. Normal sexual development goes hand in hand with that which leads to a social sense.

I have not, in this summary, taken into account the exceptional being: the creative artist. We think that a special place must be reserved for him. Cocteau, in his *Essai de Critique indirecte*, says : "A great artist is inhuman, vegetal, bestial..... . The man who creates, savagely kills everything that disturbs the paramount reflex of the instinct for preservation".

The great artist often lingers in childhood's Garden of Eden, in the unconscious, in the deep layers unknown to the outsider, from where he draws his inspiration. The psychologist is mistaken who wishes to rend the veil which protects, even more than it hides, the mystery of creation.

THE COMPLEXES

...Heureuse la créature, [1]
Qui a fait sa sépulture
Dans le ventre maternel!
Heureuse celuy, dont la vie
En sortant s'est vue ravie
Par un sommeil éternal!

JOACHIM DU BELLAY(1525-1560)
La Complainte du Désespéré

Depth psychology lays particular stress on the following factors : *complexes, repression* and *projection.*

Today, we conceive of the human psyche as an aggregate of energies in perpetual movement. It is no longer considered as a character with fixed properties, but rather with *tendencies,* (Ribot) or *functions* (Jung). Ribot distinguishes

---

(1) (translation,) ... Happy the creature
Who has built his coffin
In the womb maternal!
Happy, he whose emerging life
Is carried off in
A sleep eternal!
— *Lament of a Hopeless One*

between basic *primitive tendencies* and the *derived tendencies*. The former are common to all living beings, including animals and are strictly related to the instincts (food, sexuality). The latter shape the individualised character: generosity, avarice, openness or reserve, curiosity, a taste for travel, love of beauty, sports etc.

This notion of tendencies presupposes an inherent energy, since a tendency is a continual potentiality for acting and reacting in a preordained direction, which is triggered by the slightest appropriate stimulus. (Baudouin, *La Mobilisation de l'Enérgie*).

Psychic energy is always ready to be transformed, to be displaced from one object to another. This notion of *displacement* (Ribot's transfer) is correlative with that of tendency - exactly as the notion of the *transformation of energy* is correlative with that of its *conservation*. One represents stability, the other, variation.

The Complexes

The different tendencies of the psyche do not function in isolation, but in groups. Certain groups of interdependent tendencies are known as *complexes*. They are knots of energy, groups of ideas linked by the same affective tone: rigid entities, detached from the conscious that have fallen into the unconscious, dragging with them a great amount of psychic energy.

They are, in a sense more or less pathological nuclei, which have been detached from the evolutional stream and lead an isolated life in the psyche. They occur following traumatic shocks received in childhood, which have not been assimilated. A complex, obviously, presupposes a certain disposition, a particular sensitivity.

The complex is not only a block, an obstacle to development: it can also constitute a reserve of energies, a pivot of existence.

All human Beings have Complexes

One social class, one sex, or one period of life is no more stricken with them than another. Our era, with its conflicts between natural life and civilised life, induces the development of complexes.

As it is not possible to cover the whole subject in this work, we will simply cite the complexes most important in relation to character and will confine ourselves to those we already know can be seen in handwriting: the *inferiority complex*, the *sado-anal complex,* the *mother complex*, certain *sexual complexes*, the *guilt complex*, the *flight complex* and *narcissism.*

In order to understand the formation of the complexes, it is necessary, first of all to say a few words about *repression.*

Repression is a mechanism that causes us to forget, more or less completely, that which is painful to us, or too hard to bear, too difficult to assimilate.

That which frustrates or humiliates us, we let fall into the unconscious layers of our psyche. We do not see what we do not want to see. Nietzsche once said: "How immoral the world would seem without the faculty of forgetfulness! A poet might say that God installed forgetfulness as a doorkeeper at the threshold of the temple of human dignity" (*Humain trop Humain*).

Psychoanalysis has shown the truth of that maxim by its probings into the unconscious, explaining it with the help of dreams and the free associations connected with them.

Let us return to the origin of the *complexes*. The child has received a shock. He has suffered humiliation at the hands of a beloved person. That humiliation has been forgotten; that is to say, repressed, but, in the unconscious there is still an unhealed wound; that is the *beginning of the complex*.

The best known of all is the *inferiority complex*. Alfred Adler has emphasised its great importance in individual and social life and has placed it, together with its counterpart, the need for esteem and love, at the centre of his doctrine.

At the root of any feeling of inferiority there is often a *physical deficiency* (bad teeth, early myopia, a club-foot), or sometimes certain physical, non-pathological peculiarities that place the child apart from others, (red hair, an abnormally tall or short stature). Children who are over-dressed or poorly dressed and teased by their comrades, often fall prey to inferiority complexes.

Sometimes, however, as we have pointed out, a critical or impatient word from parents or teachers is enough to bring about a complex. Children react to humiliation in different ways, according to their temperament. One can respond to a hurtful comment on the subject of his intelligence by making a great effort, and success will eventually heal the wound.

In another, the same criticism will cause complete *discouragement*. At this point, inhibitions are formed that shackle or even paralyse development and accomplishment. Another mechanism set in motion by a psychic injury is *compensation* and *overcompensation*. Toulouse-Lautrec, who was disabled in childhood, following a fall from a horse, became a great painter of equestrian acrobats and of the circus. The little deformed creature, not content to be careful and elegant in his way of dressing, goes further and becomes a dandy. Thus the feeling of inferiority is overcompensated with vanity and pride.

When we are confronted with an inflated ego, we can almost certainly say, that there is basically a more or less hidden inferiority complex. Tendencies to denigrate others, to "pejoration," are the work of this same complex.

The complexes amass in the manner of avalanches. There is, at first, a small bit of ice: the criticism of a mother or a much loved person. The bit of ice becomes a snowball when the father or the teacher adds to it a similarly unkind remark. The snowball increases in size after a failure in an examination and becomes an avalanche following an unrequited love. And so, in time, the joyous, trusting child is transformed into a sullen mistrustful employee who thinks at every turn: "What's the good of it?" or "I'm a wash-out," thereby poisoning his own existence and that of others.

The inferiority complex, with its sinister attendants, resentment, discouragement, bitterness, jealousy, isolation, desire for revenge and its overcompensations in delusions of grandeur and mythomania, is one of humanity's greatest enemies.

This complex can, however, be cured by success, love, or by self-knowledge, which can be gained through psychoanalysis.

When the complexes are not assimilated by a healthy psyche, *neuroses* are formed. Psychic balance is constantly disturbed, the complexes draw the libido to themselves, to the detriment of mental functioning (Janet). Inhibitions which accompany the inferiority complex, shackle the individual to such a degree that he is no longer able to work as usefully as he should: he recoils from taking even minor decisions, in either his social or personal life. His whole system of relationships becomes distorted. Restraint and anxiety mar his amorous liaisons. His faculty for loving decreases, while his egocentric emotivity increases to an unhealthy degree. Some inferiority complexes can drive a person to suicide.

Nevertheless, complexes are not only negative factors, but, as Jung says, reservoirs of energy from which the individual can draw. A successful psychoanalysis achieves a dissolution of the complexes and the liberation of the energies found buried there, like unknown treasures in the depths of the soul. The way to achieve this freedom is to *become conscious*. To understand the complexes is the first step on the road to their cure.

As to *projection*, it is the exteriorisation of a subjective element and its transposition onto an object. *Everything that is unconscious is projected outward onto other persons, or onto objects outside us.* For example, our way of writing is largely a projection of our unconscious onto paper.

Still, it is wrong to believe that the individual in the grip of a complex is always desirous of being free of it. On the contrary, although suffering from its effects, frequently a person may be fond of it, nurturing and cultivating it. He parades it and is proud of it.

Let us take as an example the *sado-anal complex*. It is seen in intelligent, cultivated, eminent men, yet who are of a repulsive uncleanliness.

They jeopardise their advancement, are revolting to those around them because of their dirty fingernails, their filthy waistcoat, their nauseating odour; but, for nothing in the world would they want to change their attitude in any way.

In these cases, several elements of the complex come into play. On the one hand, there is their enjoyment of dirt, of foul odours and on the other hand, the sadistic satisfaction of their thirst for power, in forcing others to put up with their detestable habits.

A man affected by this complex cannot separate himself from his former possessions. He keeps things that no longer serve any purpose, old papers, rusty nails, jam jars, bottles. He lets foodstuffs rot rather than throw them out.

I know a librarian in a large city who so much loved the smell of the dust of old books, that he forbade his employees to air his office. One day I heard him, in a circle of friends, boasting about having dismissed an employee who had dared simply to open the window against his orders. The feeling for domination, the sadism, the love of dirt were here gathered in a very forceful combination.

I do not believe we are dealing here with an unhealthy exceptional case. We run into these individuals all the time. Psychic sadism, not reserved for this particular human type, is shown, for example, in the very common practice of *making people wait*. Men and women who always arrive late, regretful and torn with remorse, offer themselves at least three subtle satisfactions: forcing others to bow to their whims: playing a scene that, for a moment, makes them the star and finally, having themselves pardoned.

Preservation of their complexes, is also for certain people, the surest guarantee against the *void*.

The human being fears nothing so much as the void. An analyst friend once said, regarding an old woman who suffered from the fear of crossing a public square (agoraphobia): "What can you expect, she'll never rid herself of it: she has nothing but that and her pug-dog."

It is important for the graphologist to understand these mechanisms. Character has its roots in the instinctive and affective life and isolated character traits are inseparable from the totality of the personality. The same applies to *intelligence* and *artistic talents*. In music, for example, certain masters of our day, after long experience, assert that all human beings are musicians and that psychic inhibitions alone prevent them from releasing their talents. Pedagogues have observed the same thing in the field of drawing, painting and sculpture. Children who are allowed to express themselves freely, create surprising things. Psychic and instinctive inhibitions likewise shackle the development of intelligence. In whatever sphere or direction in which they can be exercised, we can ascertain either the freeing or the blocking of the personality's expressive, creative energies.

On the one hand, feelings of inferiority curb the vital impulse, the energy, the flowing of the individual's talents and faculties, and diminish his capacity for work while on the other hand, they represent a diminutions in our "feeling for community." (Adler's *Gemeinschaftsgefühl*). The feelings of inadequacy isolate a person from society, making him either apathetic or a rebel. The adolescent affected by this complex, depending upon his disposition falls into a passive or active neurosis, criminal activity being but one instance of it.

A literary work, more often than not, offers us a self-analysis by the writer. Every complex has been explored, well before being given a name. Is there any more beautiful example of the inferiority complex and its over-compensations than the *Bourgeois Gentilhomme* or *Cyrano de Bergerac*?

In *Adrienne Mesurat*, Julian Green describes the case of a projection that becomes obsessive, with its accompanying string of complexes. His *Levithian* contains several cases of projection, among others the sadistic complex of a mother who, disappointed in her marriage and detesting her husband, projects all her hatred onto her son.

I conclude this survey on the complexes with a passage that Brachfeld cites from Alfred Adler's last book, published after his death, *The Sense of Life* :

"Man would be condemned to succumb before the forces of Nature if he had not known how to use them with a view to his own ends. Who would have seriously doubted that the human individual, so poorly provided for by Mother Nature, was equipped with the feeling of inferiority which, for him, is a veritable blessing and which impels him increasingly towards a better position, towards security, towards superiority? And this enormous, although inevitable, rebellion against a feeling of inferiority inherent in man, as the basis of the development of humanity, is aroused and repeated anew in every individual's childhood... . Every move goes from imperfection to perfection."

The Complexes and their Graphic Expression

All complexes produce characteristic writing trails, groups of signs. It can be said that every complex marks the writing as much as it marks the character. One notices inhibitions in the continuity of the writing: that is to say, little joinings, new starts, or irregularities in the pressure, inflated and spasmodic strokes, certain coils. The writing becomes chopped up, too thick, too narrow, excessively expanded. There are disturbances in the rhythm, in the harmony of forms, disproportions that never increase the general level of the writing. The lowering of the "mental level," which Janet has established in neuroses, is inexorably shown in the graphic picture.

Ex. 42. - The writing of a young delinquent.

The writing is : irregular, of inferior level, sinuous, superelevated, neglected, thick, with irregular pressure. Little coiled movements, amendments, little hooks.

Neurosis, susceptibility to influence, weakness, brutality. Lying, exaggeration. Sadistic complex (pressure on the t-bars) and inferiority complex, partly overcompensated by immoderate pride (accentuated capitals and high-placed t-bars). Several signs of cunning and intelligence : the coiled movement of the "T" in "Torres" and its connection to the following letter.

The Inferiority Complex in Handwriting

Its characteristic expression is found, first, in the disproportion between the capitals and the small letters; secondly, in the disproportion between the signature and the text.

This characteristic expression of the inferiority complex is generally not the only neurotic symptom in the writing. We find it in writings of *abnormal stability* or *instability*.

C'est à Brides-les-Mains, où je me trouve

Ex. 43. - A writing marked by complexes

ou « Complexe de l'infériorité »

Ex. 44. - Inferiority Complex

In the case of *abnormal stability*, it is a matter of neurosis with *obsession*. The writing, then, is extremely rigid, often narrow and too regular. It is mechanical. The flow of the libido does not move freely. This writing expresses admirably an inhibited, fearful and constrained character. The inferiority complex is part of this neurosis and is expressed in lofty, squeezed capitals in a small, much too regular writing.

Unstable writing is rather thready, has irregular pressure, rising, descending, undulating lines, a writing trail that is irregular in height and width; briefly, every possible and imaginable irregularity. It is the writing of *more or less hysterical neurotics*, susceptible to influence, too soft, ambivalent, hypersensitive (if the pressure is light). The inferiority complex is, in these cases, expressed by exaggerated capitals (overcompensation), since pride and mythomania are part of the overcompensation of the inferiority complex. Life is not diminished, the libido is not blocked, as in the neurotic with obsessions; on the contrary, it overflows in all directions, without being centred on one object.

Ex. 45. - Melancholy. Inferiority and flight complexes.

We have already spoken about these two great neuroses with regard to the graphic expression of extraversion and introversion.

The inferiority complex, moreover, is found in almost all neuroses, in numerous guises.

The complex accomplishes its sinister designs, more particularly within the framework of the third great form of neurosis, less widespread than the others, *melancholy*.

One should not confuse this with *occasional depressions*, which are part of all neuroses and which also appear in the normal psyche. The most frequent sign of depression is the descending line.

Melancholy, a passive neurosis, of a chronic or periodic nature, is expressed in writing by the following signs: a small soft garland, lack of tension and life throughout the whole writing trail, monotony, lack of pressure. The lower extensions droop and lack any expression. Contrary to the overall writing, which is devoid of life, we sometimes find large, sharp-pointed t-bars that are directed leftwards; that is to say, toward the writer himself. These t-bars, as well as other left-tending signs, indicate the tendencies to self-destruction of the true melancholic. Often, the signature is found placed toward the left side, far from the text; sometimes, reduced to capitals only, expressing a tendency to flee from life that finds its culminating point in suicidal tendencies.

In this type of writing, the inferiority complex is no longer expressed, or scarcely at all, by the disproportionate capitals and small letters; it has taken the form of total discouragement. There is no longer any compensation or overcompensation for it, only a denial of life. The libido acts in a masochistic fashion, breaking down, so to speak, the vital tendencies.

In these latter cases, the mobilisation of energy, the transfer of the libido, are especially difficult. However, this transfer is still possible through analysis of the unconscious, enabling amazing breakthroughs which allow rekindling of the spark of life buried in the unconscious.

While on the subject of melancholy, which alternates periodically with euphoria and agitation, the *cyclothymic neurosis* should also be mentioned. I shall be speaking about it later on. Graphically, it is characterised by large garlands, by its exaggerated rightward tendency, its expansive nature and rounded forms.

Let us briefly add that *hysteria* is the exaggeration of the extraverted character, *neurosis with obsessions* the exaggeration of the introverted character. (See the chapter on the types of attitude).

In sketching the broad outlines of the different neuroses and their graphic expression, let us never forget that they are manifested most of the time as *mixed neuroses*. The hysteric has some traits of the neurotic with obsession, and vice versa.

The same is true in regard to graphic expression. We find writings that are the faithful reflection of a pure neurosis, or of a typical character as described here, but, there are many more writings that stem from mixed neuroses and show intermingling signs of both states. It is necessary to uncover the prevailing type and find the relationship between the different symptoms. We must never lose sight of the fact that, first of all, there is life, with its numerous and often unexpected manifestations and that all our evaluations are but attempts at understanding that life, which, in its richness and mobility, will always escape us.

The Sado-Anal Complex and its Expression in Handwriting

This complex pervades an individual to such a degree that we can properly speak of a *sado-anal character*. It is expressed in handwriting in a very clear way.

The most obvious sign of this character is pasty or muddy pressure, heavy, black writing.

This type of writing contains signs of aggressiveness: sharp-pointed finals, clubbed t-bars. The writing is often angular (but not always).

Ex. 46. - Anal Complex.

Ex. 47. - Anal Complex, aggressiveness, spirit of revenge.

Other signs: the letters "a", "d," "q," are split up into two parts.

The writing is often small and disconnected. It fills the whole page without any ventilation, thus giving a very material impression.

Another type of this character: the writing is squeezed, rigid, too regular, too connected, with signs of despotism, such as exaggerated t-bars, triangular lower loops.

Generally, several of these symptoms are manifested together and form a syndrome.

It goes without saying that all misers, more or less, belong to this group.

This complex can be found in all degrees of intensity in any type of individual and in this respect relates to a partial regression to an infantile stage.

Ex. 48. - Anal Complex, avarice

Ex. 49. - Anal complex, sexual complexes

This description does not exclude other manifestations of this type. For example, in the case of an aesthete, the outer mask that represents the overcompensation of his complexes hides the fundamental primitive, tendencies; or, in the case of a scholar with Thinking as the main function, the primordial tendencies will be hidden. An exaggerated cleanliness (the subject is obsessed with the idea of washing himself: he washes his hands every minute) often hides a repressed complex.

Julius Streicher's handwriting is an excellent illustration of the anal-sadistic type.

This writing is angular, of average size, with prolonged upper and lower extensions, connected, rigid, right-slanted, vulgar, excessively double-joined.

But, what is most striking and of particular interest, is its very low level, its childish appearance and its precision. The very strong, sometimes muddy pressure is symptomatic. The extreme rigidity of the writing (see the first, clubbed downstroke of the signature), the sharp-pointed finals, perfectly express sadism.

We all know who Streicher is, one of the great war criminals, a notorious sadist.

He is a fanatic, inaccessible to reason. The complex has become the dominant factor of his life. It is no *longer just a complex*. He is obsessive, a sick man, yet fully responsible. It is believed that Streicher, before he found his vocation as an executioner of the Jews, was a schoolmaster and a tormentor of the children too, no doubt.

When a graphologist studies the handwriting of a well known person, it is hard to be totally objective about the writer. Let us try here to find again the known qualities of the writing: explosive temper is reflected in the writing, which is at the same time angular, heavily pressured and right-slanted: fanaticism is shown, in the black, thin, compact

Ex. 50. - Julius Streicher's writing. Anal complex, sadism

and over-connected strokes. Nothing can enter into this closed circle of ideas, no influence that could moderate or soften the inexorable methodicalness of such an individual.

Again, we find all the characteristics of the anal complex: its dirtiness, expressed in the muddy patches; the sadism, in the writing's extreme rigidity and harsh angles; the sense of power, in the triangular lower extensions and in the immoderate size of the signature.

The sense of order, pushed to the point of mania, is found again in the writing's regularity. Extreme egoism is seen in the angles and the reversed strokes, as well as duplicity and deceit in the covered strokes, leftward tendencies and double joins.

This man, devoid of any human feeling, is not lacking in intelligence. This is expressed in the progressive strokes joining the "d's" to the next letter in the word. The angular and right-slanted writing denotes an active temperament.

The leftward tendency is here particularly manifested in the accents: the small horizontal strokes, which in German script, indicate the duplication of the consonants "n" and "m", are executed as left-tending curves (see line 2, *dann*; line 3, *kommen* and *wenn*), while the semicircle over the "u" is a completely closed circle (line 4 : *Teufel* and *niedergerungen*, and line 5 : *Teufel*). In addition to this, the letters are so double-joined that they become unrecognisable, such as the final "r" detached from the signature.

It is interesting at this point, to read the document. Graphologists generally abstain from reading a text, fearing to be misled. However, in the present case, let us approach it from both the graphological and psychological point of view, and look at the meaning of its text: "Humanity will have attained happiness and peace only when the devil has been vanquished. The devil is the Jew".

Streicher thus projects his own "shadow" onto the Jews. In identifying the Jew with the Devil, the spirit of evil, this projection assumes colossal proportions.

The handwriting of a *businessman* supplies us with another illustration of the anal complex.

Ex. 51. - A businessman's writing.

We all recognise this type of writing, vulgar, hard and childish. We have all met the human type to which this writing corresponds: a man who is vulgar, "a cad," a crank, miserly, embittered and crafty.

The dominant traits of this handwriting are: its rigidity, inky strokes, sharp pressure with congested letters filled with ink; its irregularity, amendments, pointed finals and lower extensions, aggressive t-bars, and numerous superelevations. The writing is either vertical or left-slanted, thus full of ambivalence.

Something ugly, dirty, unpleasant is emitted by this writing. In fact, the writer was described to me by those around him as a dirty, careless person.

The writer is a neurotic whose neurosis has become one with his character.

In other words, what we describe as avarice, acute egoism, spitefulness, the character of one who is a "difficult person", is the description of an "anal complex". It is the result of an inadequate upbringing, an unsuccessful adjustment in early childhood. Such an individual's first reaction is to defend himself. He is aggressive and possessive and has not made the necessary transition from egocentric behaviour to socially acceptable behaviour.

This writing reflects a strong will, a strict discipline that the writer imposes on himself, despite a deep-seated instability (note, on the one hand, the angular, semi-arcadic strokes and on the other, the writing's irregularity. We are dealing with a worker who is stubborn, tireless, meticulous, fanatical, but totally lacking in spontaneity. His life is a succession of mechanical acts.

He is economical, miserly and loves money. If he should happen to make a generous gesture, it is will only be out of self-interest or snobbery.

He is proud and ambitious, at the mercy of his inferiority complex.

His criticism is harsh and bruising; he feels a need to demolish others, believing that this is the best way to assert his superiority.

He is sensual, but incapable of loving and wants to possess without giving.

A difficult colleague, he creates enmity in all quarters. Although he denigrates others, he is himself vulnerable in this respect.

He is a spiteful, rancorous character, bent on revenge.

Although his intelligence is only average, he is reflective, prudent and distrustful. His behaviour reflects the pressures of his sadism and fear.

He has practical sense; he knows how to calculate. Stubborn, tenacious, wishing to dominate, he would know how to make himself indispensable in the position he holds, for he is aware of the secrets of the business and therefore wields a certain power. Everyone detests and fears him.

Rich, an old bachelor, he lives alone and deprives himself of everything in order to amass money.

OTHER COMPLEXES

The Mother Complex

For some individuals, the first love, mother love remains attached to its original object and is never redirected. For neurotics, the weak and the unbalanced, all their inner drives, including their sexual ones, are fixated on the mother.

However, it is not only his infantile sexuality that fixates the neurotic on his mother, but his need for protection, for "mother" represents security.

In moments of extreme danger, a man's thoughts turn toward the one who protected him in his infancy. The soldier dying on the battlefield, the condemned man about to be executed, will cry out: "Mama!"

The *mother complex* is not shown by a single sign. It is a combination of signs indicating weakness, neurosis and inhibition, with a general regressive tendency; or else childishness in the form and organisation leading one to conclude that this complex is present in the character of a man or woman.

Ex. 52. - Complexes of a sexual nature, inhibitions.

Ex. 53. - Sexual complexes, erotomania, obsessive ideas.

Ex. 54. - Guilt complex

Sexual Complexes

Sexual complexes are expressed in handwriting by several signs or groups of signs. However, it is particularly in the lower extensions that their manifestations are given free rein. Bizarre forms, inflated loops exaggerated triangles, breaks, lower extensions that are too large, or atrophied, indicate disturbances of a sexual nature.

A too heavy or too light pressure, spasmodic strokes of all kinds repeated in a writing trail, are equally revealing. (see Exs. 52 and 53).

Guilt Complex

As to the *guilt complex*, it is revealed in the writing by all the symptoms of *fear*. Inhibitions of different kinds, extreme smallness, or squeezing of the writing can indicate guilt feelings. This complex and its graphic manifestations often go together with an inferiority complex and regression in general.

Ex. 55. Flight complex

Flight Complex

The *flight complex* is expressed primarily by a filiform and sinuous writing trail, often light. The writer flees from responsibilities and goes back on decisions without being able to assume a definite stance.

Narcissism

Narcissism shows itself in different ways, in behaviour as well as in handwriting.

This auto-eroticism is easy to recognise in banal writings, where it is expressed in a naïve and gross manner by exaggerated capitals, embellished and artificial writing.

It is more difficult to uncover this in handwritings of a superior level, in which the writer of good taste avoids any showy signs. Nevertheless, the scholar, or man of letters, while on the whole capable of concealing his narcissism in certain details of conversation, cannot control its appearance in his handwriting, which is simple, combined, rhythmic, a bit too rounded, having regressive curves (directed towards the ego) with a slightly affected grace, in which his self-love is revealed.

Everything we call a *character trait*: courage, cowardice, pride, modesty, avarice, generosity, an open or closed character, fear, lying, laziness, assumes a new meaning in the light of depth psychology, for complexes very often shape the basis of an individual's characteristic properties. We can easily understand that timidity as well as cowardice may be a consequence of an inferiority complex. We have already seen the formation of what we call avarice.

Lying

Let us look more closely at *lying*. A child may have a tendency to lie, either through fear of being mistreated or as a result of mythomania.

Lying through fear is part of the inferiority complex and the guilt complex. What we call mythomania is part of the hysterical character which was studied with regard to extraversion. Lying through fear often appertains to the introverted character, because of the difficulties with expression that characterise this type.

Mythomania

As to *mythomania* : children often do not know how to distinguish between truth and imagination. Much more than adults, they live in their unconscious and what seems false to adults has truth in their eyes.

Laziness

Laziness can have different roots. It can disappear following a mobilisation of psychic energy, an awakening of dormant energies.

We will see, in the course of this work, to what degree psychoanalytical ideas change our attitude toward a character who, for us, is a sum total of vibrant energies.

Dispersion

Dispersion, lack of concentration, can likewise be due to a lack of interest in a thing and can be transformed by the awakening of an interest that concentrates the attention. When a graphologist establishes a deficiency of this nature in the handwriting of a child or an adult, he will do well not only to note the existence of this shortcoming, but to point out the possible displacement of energy and, in describing the ailment, suggest the remedy.

ANIMA AND ANIMUS

The Problem of the Sexes

The psychological concepts expounded up to this point belong to the realm of general experience, and are more or less accessible to every individual. On the other hand, we have hardly glimpsed the unknown world of the unconscious. It is by virtue of the exploration of dreams by depth psychology that we know about its activity, which, although invisible, is nonetheless influential. We have already established the contrasts inherent in the human soul. One of the most marked contrasts of our psyche resides in what Jung calls the *images of the soul*, the "Anima" and the "Animus". This notion needs to be studied under two aspects: the conscious and the unconscious, the inner and the outer life.

The basic masculine-feminine polarity is, during the course of life, revealed in an infinite variety of ways. In many cases, this duality creates no difficulty. A slight tension first experienced as a result of the attraction of two persons of the opposite sex, leads on to coupling, procreation and union in an unconscious compensation. The life of the couple is ruled according to biological and social laws. However, for other individuals, love becomes a problem, the central problem of life.

We see women madly in love with a man whom they cannot do without, even if separation is forced upon them, and men torn between two women without being able to come to a decision. Neither will power nor reason can pull them out of a situation which they cannot resolve.

If the effects of sexual passion have been known since time immemorial, their true causes escape the majority of human beings. When consulted by people in moments of crises hoping for enlightened advice, the graphologist should make sure that he has a good grasp of the underlying factors in the emotional problems faced by his clients.

The attraction between man and woman is, needless to say of a sexual nature, but a partner is not chosen simply for the greatest physical satisfaction and even less so for procreative capacity. Beauty often attracts in an irresistible way, but ugliness also has its attractions. We admire sparkling intellectual and artistic gifts, but many self-effacing persons, without apparent talent, find worshippers. The world is often surprised and cannot understand the reasons for certain amorous liaisons, why an average man could inspire such lively passion in women, or how a woman without charm can seduce a man who appears to be superior to her in every way.

In its early stages, psychoanalysis taught that the love-object, for a man, replaces either the mother or sister; and in the case of a woman, the father or the brother. However, that interpretation does not explain the phenomenon in all its complexity. It sheds light on only one part of it. Certainly, the attachment of the son for the mother and the unconscious projection of the mother onto the beloved object, is a very influential psychic factor. Yet, there are also other elements that come into play. Jung explains this complicated process by his concept of *the image of the soul.*

The latter is composed of three elements; in the man, it arises through the image of the *mother,* who is, for him, the first impression of woman, his first great love. For the woman, it is the *father* who evokes and carries the image of the soul. These ideal images will be modified by *subsequent encounters* with other men and women during childhood and adolescence; but they are also *shaped beforehand* in our unconscious by the reflection of *ancestral experiences* that we carry within us. Here we find one of the archetypal moulds in which the individual life is cast.

For, just as we inherit a body and physiological functions adapted to the exigencies and struggles of life, we inherit a strongly differentiated mental structure, which has nothing to do with our personal experience. A human being born now has a brain ready to function in a typically human fashion and particularly in a way specific to our era. Our psychic edifice is based on foundations that are as old as the human race. It is from those ages, lost in the mists of time, that the archetypal representations date, which will be discussed in due course.

Thus, one of the images that lives in us is the image of the soul, that of woman in man, and man in woman. As soon as this image is awakened, as soon as we meet a person bearing traits essentially similar to those of the living image within us, the relationship is born. Whether it be fashioned by love, by hate or by fear, it will always be forceful, irresistible and magical.

Many individuals, especially men, recoil, as if in terror, from this attraction that the image of the soul exerts. They feel that in it there is something stronger than themselves, which threatens to upset the balance of their life. They take flight, hurting the women who represent their Anima and take refuge in others who are only females to them, objects of physical love, with whom they have no deep contact.

Others, on the contrary, cannot live without the projection of this psychic entity. As soon as one amorous liaison comes to an end, they project their inner image, Anima or Animus, onto another object, man or woman. Thus, many individuals' lives are but a perpetual chain of projections by means of which they exteriorise their innermost being, preventing them from ever finding fulfilment in themselves.

The projection of the Anima and of the Animus is a source of happiness, *the* source of happiness, an experience we have all had.

However, it is equally a source of endless misunderstanding, for the unconscious projection causes one to see in the person one thinks one loves a part of oneself, rather than the real person. We project onto the other elements of self : we clothe him in a character that, in truth, he does not possess.

The unconscious fusion of two beings, by virtue of the links of projection, can be very close, but it is inevitably put to the test. It is fatal when the partners, or even just one of them, realises that the true character of the beloved does not correspond to what he thought he had seen in that person.

The beloved object, and the projection with which we embellish it, are all the more different from each other when the image of the soul is rather remote from present-day romantic and archetypal images. The woman whose Animus wears the disguise of a Dutch phantom, a Parsifal, or a warrior hero, cannot rediscover those characteristics in a modern man.

It so happens that, in projecting onto the beloved being the ideal we carry within us, we unconsciously oblige the person to conform to that ideal. There are women who wear themselves out in distorting their spontaneous reactions the better to incorporate the Anima of the man they love.

For his part, the man whose Anima evokes the figure of an infinitely maternal woman, representing Mother Nature's inexhaustible love, will be profoundly disappointed to find in his spouse only the mean and possessive love of a mediocre woman. If he carries within him the archetypal image of a fairy or a sorceress, he will fall in love with a *femme fatale*, an actress or a movie star. It is possible for an intelligent, sensitive young man, unconsciously obsessed by another archetype to pick up an ordinary girl from a brothel, seeing in her a courtesan of Plato's time. The magic that emanates from the image of the soul can be stronger than any prejudices, traditions, logic or good sense.

The reflections of the powerful images of the Anima and the Animus may be encountered at any moment. They appear in our dreams as fairies, sorceresses, prostitutes in a man; as a magician, a conquering hero [1] in a woman, or under a thousand other aspects. Very often, during dreams, the image of the soul is projected onto a person of the man or woman's immediate circle. Dream analysis reveals the psychological nature of the projections and distinguishes the projection from the real being as bearer of the image.

Let us consider another aspect of this very complex matter: the Anima and the Animus do not act simply as projections, or as links that tie us to other beings, but they also act at the very heart of our psyche.

Every individual is bisexual. Physiologically, this is explained by the fact that each one of us descends from a mother and a father who have provided us with feminine and masculine elements. The opposite pole to the visible gender remains latent and unconscious, but is no less active for that. It contributes abundantly toward the make-up of our psychic being, our character. We therefore carry within us our opposite pole, masculine or feminine, as an image and as a quality of character. In a man, the Anima will constitute his

---

(1) The cosmonaut, particularly, attracts to himself the Animus of the modern woman, as well as the popular singer.

unconscious femininity, inferior to his conscious masculinity; it is a sort of archaic, uncontrolled femininity, a rudimentary or overwhelming emotivity, a kind of capricious Eros. In a woman, the Animus is revealed as an intellectuality that is often simplistic and illogical, a Logos of an inferior kind. These concepts also help to elucidate a problem that has never ceased to preoccupy graphologists and to perplex the public: *whether it is possible to recognise a writer's sex.*

There are men, obsessed by their Anima, in whom it is manifested in all the deeds and gestures of their life, much more than their virility.

Take for example, first of all, homosexuals who, even in the realm of sexuality properly speaking, maintain a feminine attitude. In them, it is the Anima that is conscious, whereas they project their unconscious virility in the domain of Love. These men are as capricious as women, whimsical, sentimental, gossipy, often very gifted in the domain of art, fashion, or literature. They dress effeminately, like to sew, keep house, and all feminine pastimes. It is not surprising that their writing assumes the appearance of feminine handwriting.

But, apart from these extreme cases, many men are under the sway of their latent, more or less unconscious femininity, which is not shown generally in their everyday life, but only in particular areas. It occurs in many artists who, while remaining quite normal in their sexual life, are very sensitive to the "messages" of their Anima, a sensitivity that justly explains their creative talent. The artist's Muse is his inspirational Anima. Men's handwriting, in general, is smaller than that of women, while in those whose Anima plays a preponderant role, it is often large, rounded, with triangular lower extensions, or other features characteristic of feminine writing.

In women, unconscious maleness can be a burning problem. Many of them would prefer to keep to a feminine role, but, compelled by inner drives, they choose a profession that puts them in competition with men in the battle of life and to earn a living. It is natural for their handwriting then to assume more virile features. It becomes harder and more angular when it is a question of occupations that require energy and faculties for organisation; or else small, rounded, simplified, if it is the intellectual faculties that are developed.

The problem of the Anima is too complex to be dealt with in depth in this work.

The woman who has a marked masculine component is intelligent, energetic, enterprising, loyal and firm in character, but the Animus often makes her stubborn and aggressive.

The woman's masculinity, easily destructive when it remains unconscious, can develop, as the result of intense inner work during psychoanalysis, to the point of becoming a superior function which then fulfils the role of "inner guide" [1].

To come back to handwritings, it is therefore, difficult to recognise sex in a handwriting, for *the writing reflects the psychological sex* and not the physiological sex of the writer.

It is not easy to understand and to accept the psychological theories expounded above, when they have not been supported by personal experiences, such as discoveries made when undergoing analysis.

The image of the soul, which could also be called a psychological complex, is simultaneously *image and function*. The literature of all peoples teems with manifestations of the Anima and the Animus. They animate almost the whole of

---

(1) I refer the reader to Jung's works and to my *Symbolisme du Rêve*, in which he describes the evolution of several women and the important role that their Animus plays in their daily life and in their dream life.

dramatic and cinematographic art. Depth Psychology has
studied and expressed what poets have always understood.
We find a classic representation of the Anima in Dante's
Beatrice. The *Divine Comedy* is a grandiose representation
of the human unconscious in the age of the Renaissance, and
it is the Anima that, in the person of Beatrice, leads the poet
into the unknown spheres. Charles Morgan, in *The Flashing
Stream*, presents the Anima of a modern man and its inspirational role. H.G. Wells grapples with the complicated
problem of a woman possessed by her Animus in the heroine
of *Christina Alberta's Father.*

Ex. 56. - A man's "Anima" writing.

Ex. 57. - A man's "Anima" writing.

Ex. 58. - A woman's "Animus" writing.

Two human beings, during a happy marriage, can remain for many years in that unconscious fusion we call "mystical participation". But life sometimes destroys that union. The illusion on which it rested is unveiled, the projection is then withdrawn from one of the partners. Take the case of two disconcerted individuals, shaken in their equilibrium, who ask advice of a psychologist: life has lost its charm because of the departure of a beloved person, or because of the breakdown of an unconscious participation. The individual is obliged to make a complete about-turn and to redirect the libido invested in that union. It is here that psychological discernment can be of help. It is a matter of distinguishing between the projected image of the soul and the true personality of the partner, and then to find a new *modus vivendi* based on the understanding of the two souls rather than on an illusion.

In the case of an irrevocable parting, individuals will have to create for themselves an independent and, for some time at least, a solitary life. If they have enough strength of soul, they will perhaps find in introspection the means of re-animating hidden centres. Neglect, despair can lead them to an inner development and to the revelation of their deeper personality. We touch here upon the problem of individuation.

INDIVIDUATION

Discovery of the Self

We are indebted to C.G. Jung for his discovery that introspection, pursued through the unconscious, manifested in dreams, can lead to a spiritual evolution in ways known from all eternity, such as Yoga or ancient initiation rituals. [1] In the course of this evolution, the core of the psychic substance is displaced: the empirical Ego, subjective, under the influence of the personal life, is recreated around a new centre. The whole personality is transformed.

This transformation is produced by virtue of a profound penetration of the conscious to the obscure layers of the unconscious. The latter then becomes apparent to the individual's clear consciousness. The conscious and the unconscious, so often in contradiction, are joined in a new orientation, a new harmony, in which the individual finds a feeling of plenitude. Sources of energy, of creativity, of happiness, until now unknown, are revealed to him, for man

---

(1) C.G.Jung : *L'Homme à la Découverte de son Ame, L'Homme et ses Symboles*

does not repress only what is painful and inferior in his nature, but often the best of himself.

The interest up to now devoted to the realistic discovery of the world or acquiring possessions from it, is withdrawn more and more toward the invisible centre of the personality, the Self or higher Ego. In the course of its displacement, the psychic energy is never cut off or repressed, but is led into another layer. The Self, by the magnetism that is proper to it, attracts the libido and becomes more and more detached from the other psychic elements. The individual, often to his own surprise, gains in objectivity. He acquires a distance from himself, he rises above his own contradictions and sentimental or other conflicts, which, in themselves, seemed insoluble.

The Self, the powerful centre that is not constructed but reveals itself, is represented in Hindu philosophy as a block of salt.

Among its many symbols, can be cited: the Swan, the Lotus Flower, the Crystal, the invincible Fortress, the Golden Flower. In Christianity, it is Christ who becomes the new centre of the human soul: St. Paul expresses it in these words: "It is no longer I, it is Christ who lives in me". Every being who has undergone a spiritual revelation knows this reversal of values and the channelling of his interest down a new path.

Henceforth, the empirical Ego, with its desires, its fears, all the manifestations of the affective life, yields more and more to a centre of potentiality that creates an atmosphere of serenity and calm which irradiates the new being. Life's rhythm is changed; Anima and Animus lose their obsessive character.

They are transformed or are projected onto a superior being: for the monk, it is the Madonna: for the nun, it is Christ. The symbols vary according to the country, the

16308

✝

CARITAS

Tamanrasset. 22.7.14

Cher Monsieur

merci de votre si affectueuse lettre du
23 mai ainsi que de l'article très trop
bienveillant & trop flatteur & de la Revue
indigène. Je suis ne ne peut plus touché
& reconnaissant de votre si cordiale &
fidèle amitié.

Ex. 59. - Father de Foucauld's writing.

religion, the philosophy, the civilisation in which the individual is raised, but the psychological process remains the same.

Graphologists, to my knowledge, have never tried to uncover the Self in handwriting, with the exception of Magnat, who, in his beautiful book, *Poésie de l'Ecriture*, approaches this problem. Yet that illumination is present, it asserts itself, and can be revealed in the psychic content or equally in the psychological functions, in behaviour, in masculinity or femininity [1].

In what way will this Self, so difficult to understand, more difficult still to realise in one's life, be shown in handwriting?

I believe that the Self is shown by the *general level*, which is expressed particularly by the rhythm and genuine originality of the forms. Let one here express a hypothesis that will appear strange and contradictory to some principles of graphology : *the Self should be seen by the absence of certain signs.*

Let me explain : the Self is shown precisely in life by the absence of egoism, pride, "pushiness," overactivity, distrust, fear. The Self is revealed little by little as the empirical Ego is effaced. The more the internal polarities - masculinity-femininity, passivity-activity, love-hate, extraversion-introversion, etc., are lessened or effaced, the more evident and real the Self becomes. It is this Self, not the outward personality, which contains the secret of true superiority.

The more the writing loses its large, exaggerated strokes, its loops and paraphs, its heaviness and precipitation, all expressions of the empirical Ego and consequently of pride and egoism, and the more simplified and harmonious the writing becomes, while still remaining alive and expressive,

---

(1) Pulver talks at length about the Self in his book, *Personne, Caractère, Destin*, which does not study the question from a graphological angle.

the closer we get to discovering the Self. (see Father de Foucauld's writing, Ex. 59).

Perhaps this interpretation, which I offer with every reservation, allows us to understand the "general level" of a handwriting, the subject of so much debate in graphology. The originality, the fullness and richness of the personality do not suffice to explain the value of a writing's general level. It is only the concept of the Self, as the impersonal governor of the totality of the psyche, which will indicate the true origin of the superior, average or inferior aspect of a writing.

Obviously, this applies only to fully organised writings in which the writer is in possession of all means of expression. We do not deny that people exist who are in harmony with their inner Self, whose writing does not, however, show a high general level. This is because the writer is impeded in his means of graphic expression. Here again we touch upon the limitations of graphology, which it would be presumptuous to disregard [1].

The preceding remarks should not discourage the graphologist. The psychological theories that we have tried to summarise can only produce a general atmosphere of understanding and allow the possibility of working in greater depth.

---

(1) We must not confuse the Self with the Superego of Freudian psychoanalysis. Freud's Superego (Über-Ich) is formed in the child at the beginning of the latency stage, which I sketched in the chapter on the "Formation of the Character". At that time, the child "desexualises" his attachments to the mother or father and replaces them by an identification with the parents. The parents' authority is no longer experienced as coming from the outside: it is "interiorised", thus forming the child's *moral conscience* : "this is good, this is forbidden". The Superego maintains the severe character, the authority that the child attributed to his parents and teachers. It can lead the individual into painful tensions between the Ego, its desires and needs and the immutable ideal imposed by the Superego.

The more that a graphologist is initiated into the many problems of psychology, the better he will understand the true essence of a being through its many manifestations.

The details to be studied, as much from the graphic as from the psychological side, should never cause us to lose sight of the whole.

They should, on the contrary, serve us in supporting our syntheses. In psychology, *a whole is always greater than the sum of its parts*. It is this principle that will guide us in the second part of this work, which is more specifically devoted to practical graphology.

PART TWO

THE SYMBOLISM OF SPACE
AND THE DEVELOPMENT OF
HANDWRITING

Symbolism of the Zones and Directions

Handwriting analysis is an act of comprehension and interpretation; it is thereby, allied to psychoanalysis. A *comprehensive* analysis is different from *causal* analysis, which seeks the source of a given factor. The first interprets a psychological fact, seeking out *what it means*, what purpose it aims at. Alfred Adler gave to psychological investigation the name of "final analysis".

Let us apply this concept to graphology by saying that every movement, every human gesture is charged with meaning and all come together to express the totality of the personality.

When one studies facial expressions, one can see fury, pain or joy, without having to reflect on the causal links between the moving forms of the features and what they express. It is enough to grasp instinctively and intuitively what the face expresses. We understand whether a smile is affected or sincere, but would be unable to say what muscular contractions or combination of contractions produces the nuance between the sincere smile and the affected smile.

The graphologist who understands another's psyche though the medium of handwriting, can arrive at understanding without realising the source of the image before his eyes, without being concerned as to its mechanical basis. It is certainly of great interest for him to study the physiological conditions of the writing, but it is not essential to producing a good analysis. The interpretation of a writing is based on the image as it is presented and not on the conditions that are at its source. The writing speaks directly to him who contemplates it, much as a smile does, or the shape of a hand.

Handwriting, which has been referred to as "frozen movement", is essentially dynamic.

It is one of the most spontaneous expressions of the psyche's activity. It is important to understand that the scriptural movement is composed of two different elements : *movements of conscious origin and movements of unconscious origin.*

The conscious intentions, or the desire to produce a certain effect (Klages' *Leitbild* or guiding image), can lead the writer, for example, to adopt an ostentatious writing, or to imitate the writing of a person he admires; but, in spite of himself, unconscious elements slip into the writing trail in the form of little signs of inhibition. Crépieux-Jamin, in his *ABC de la Graphologie*, observed very accurately that the little signs, insignificant in appearance, have more import than the gaudy forms of the large letters. He did not, however, make a distinction between the conscious and unconscious elements in the writing. Max Pulver, on the basis of psychoanalytical concepts, insists a great deal on that distinction. (also, see Magnat : *Poésie de l'Ecriture*).

Emanations from the conscious and the unconscious interpenetrate each other in the act of writing, in much the same way as elements of a collective and individual nature do. *Projection*, particularly, plays a role of the first rank in this instance. *Every unconscious psychic element*, Jung asserts, *is projected outward*.

Let us recall what was said, at the beginning of this work, on the subject of the *symbolic nature* of handwriting. When writing, we project onto the paper symbolic forms, which, being alive within us, express our inner life. Or, more precisely, we modify the traditional, calligraphic forms, according to the conscious ideas and the unconscious images that determine our personality.

Every unconscious production is based on these same assumptions; that is to say, in our mind's eye, every psychic representation occupies a certain position in space.

Both in dreams and in handwriting, the same archetypical representations and the same *symbolism of space* appear.

At the very moment of writing, we are positioning ourselves in space. The sheet of paper represents the world in which we evolve and every scriptural movement is symbolic of our behaviour in that world.

The gliding from *left to right* that we impose on the pen is a symbolic movement, which we no longer consciously conceive of as such, but which can be explained by the successive stages of the evolution of humanity. In the beginning, and even today in Hebraic writing, this movement was accomplished from right to left, and the gesture from left to right, which has become natural to us, was introduced into writing by the *Greeks*. It is they, also, who adopted *the horizontal line*, a material or imaginary line that symbolises the earth.

Bachofen, the Swiss Hellenist scholar, explains, in his *Symbolisme des Sépultures*, the meaning of the right side and the left side. Since time began the *left* has expressed *the passive, feminine principle*, the *right, the active, masculine principle*. For him, when some sacred horns on an altar on Delos were transferred from the left to the right side as related by Plutarch, this marked the transition from the aphrodisiacal, feminine principle to the apollonian, masculine principle. "Magical power resides in the left hand, terrestrial power, in the right hand; the left belongs to the feminine and passive potential, the right to the masculine and active potential of nature". Bachofen demonstrates that one always discovers in matriarchal civilisations the idea of the superiority of the left side, while in the patriarchal civilisations it is the right side that is considered superior.

Every *leftward movement* symbolises a return inward, the past, meditation or, in a very broad, unconcretised sense, towards the mother.

The symbolism of the right and the left is archaic and archetypal. The symbolism of the left side embraces what, since time immemorial, has been associated with the feminine principle : passivity, receptivity, attachment to the earth, tenacity, maternity, spirit of preservation, love and feeling. Every rightward movement expresses activity, combative tendencies, the desire for conquest, the spirit of enterprise. The right expresses the tendency towards the future, towards others, towards the world. We accord, to the right and to the left, the meanings of extraversion and introversion, with the numerous associations attaching to that.

It can also be said, that rightward movement represents a gesture moving away from the writer's body, symbolically from the Ego (the empirical and individual Ego), while movement directed leftwards represents a return toward the Ego. Hence the whole gamut of right and left-tending writings, to which graphology has always attributed the meaning of activity or passivity, altruism or egoism, which can be added to the images of the collective unconscious.

With the symbolism of the right and the left is associated the symbolism *of above and below, of height and depth.*

This symbolism is widespread throughout the world, with only slight nuances of meaning that vary according to the basic religious and mythical concepts of different peoples and civilisations. Humanity has always conceived of the upper world as ruled by gods and angels and the lower world as the domain of devils and demons.

Our language is filled with the symbolism of space. We cannot do otherwise than picture to ourselves spirit above and matter below. Just as we believe that God, pure spirit, is everywhere, that He is the All, inevitably we picture *the spirit as being above us in space.*

It is therefore quite natural that, in our dreams as well as in handwriting, a movement upward represents a symbolic movement toward spirit.

Above therefore, embraces every ancient and modern representation of the celestial, the divine and the sublime, of distinction, success, of growth and of light. The thrust upward indicates ascension, as much from the moral as the social point of view.

Below, from the spiritual, moral and social point of view, represents the abyss. The idea of *below* is filled with pejorative and baleful connotations (a man fallen very low), with signs of pessimism, fatigue, nervous depression, decadence, downfall, vice and crime (the *dregs* of humanity). The *depth* has yet another meaning: one speaks of a profound soul, a profound mind, a profound feeling. A *descent into the depths* can also mean a descent into one's own unconscious. The hidden treasures of legends are found in the depths of the earth or the sea.

According to Bachofen, the earth, the maternal breast, is inseparably joined to everything that has to do with procreation and sexuality. For the ancients, the act of ploughing the earth and depositing the seed upon it, was identified with the sexual act. It is therefore entirely natural that a movement downward symbolises not only a tendency toward the material, but also instinctive tendencies and sexual impulses.

Let us now apply our symbolic concepts to handwriting. Our present alphabetical system is comprised of three zones: *the upper zone : upper extensions, the middle zone : body of the letters and or interior letters and the lower zone : lower extensions.*

Even in the early days of graphology the symbolism of these three zones applied, the upper extensions being seen as the abode of the spirit, the middle zone as the abode of the soul and the lower extensions as the area of the body and the instinctive tendencies.

To use modern terminology, the upper zone indicates intellectual and spiritual aspirations, the middle zone the affective impulses and the lower zone the material, realistic and sexual tendencies.

By combining the meanings of the right side and the left side and of the superimposed three zones, we succeed in forming a framework that will serve as a basis for our analysis of writing. Pulver places this system of movements, this topography of the psychic zones, at the centre of his graphology (*Symbolik der Handschrift*). An earlier, much more primitive scheme of the zones and directions had been produced by Duparchy-Jeannez in his *Essai de graphologie scientifique.*

This same scheme could serve as the basis for the sketching in of a topographical map of the soul. If reminds one of the symbolism in many of the drawings of dreams executed by subjects during the course of psychoanalytical treatment.

It is within these different zones and directions that the libido evolves. Psychic energy is manifested in its extensive or intensive tendencies: intellectual or materialistic, speculative or realistic. According to the intensity of the direction of that energy, one or the other of the zones and direction of the writing will be fuller and more animated.

However, the preceding considerations would be idle speculation on the part of the graphologist, if experience did not bear them out. In fact, people with active natures, drawn to the outside world, represented by the right side, write in a more right-tending way than passive people and intellectuals, who, according to graphologists, have a tendency to develop the upper extensions more than materialistic people. Extraverts generally adopt a more right-slanted and more spread-out writing than introverts.

This concept of the three zones and the two directions enlightens the graphologist who, in consequence is able not only to understand a handwriting more fully, but can interpret the graphic signs for himself, without having to learn their interpretations by heart. The symbolism of the *right* side gives us the meaning of spread-out or progressive writing. The symbolism of the *above* and the *below* helps us to understand the meaning of prolonged writing. Obviously, these verifications do not exclude the detailed study of each writing, but they make the writing more alive and, at the same time, provide a solid basis for the graphologist's intuition.

All symbolism is rich in nuances and multiple in its facets. A paraph, for example, which evolves in the lower zone, can indicate, according to the diverse meanings connected with this zone, either a preponderance of sexual tendencies or a moral downfall. High-placed accents can express intuitive propensities, spiritual aspirations, as well as a lack of sense of reality. It is, in each case, imperative to study the various possibilities of interpretation, but the guiding line remains the same: a movement upward indicates a tendency toward the heights of an intellectual, spiritual or social nature; a movement downward indicates the tendencies that correspond to the symbolism of the *below*.

As always, *the writing as a whole, including the general level*, determines the detail, and as a result, the nuances in the interpretation of the zones and the directions. The graphologist's intuition will help him to choose between the various meanings of the same symbol. This *framework of zones and directions* should always be kept in mind by the graphologist, who should apply their meaning not only to the whole of the writing, but also to each letter. *The envelope with the address*, when seen from the angle of symbolic graphology, offers a special field of observation, as Pulver has demonstrated, as well as the *placement and direction of the signature*. All the interpretations given by graphologists (flight from life, premeditated suicide) on the subject of signatures placed to the left of the vertical axis on the sheet of paper (Duparchy-Jeannez), fall perfectly within the framework of the symbolism of handwriting.

Symbolism of the Zones and Directions

The Heights
Upper Zone :
Intellectuality
Spirituality
Aspirations, ambition

Introversion

Passivity
Femininity
Past
I

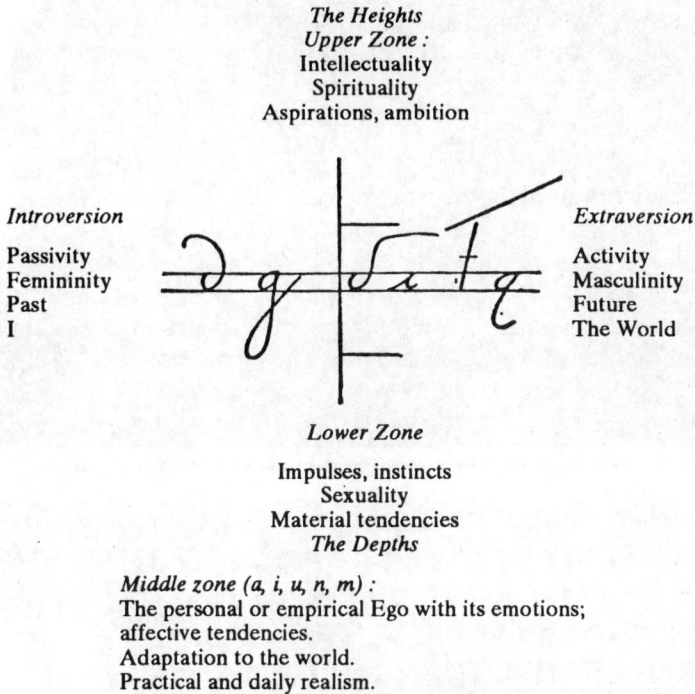

Extraversion

Activity
Masculinity
Future
The World

Lower Zone

Impulses, instincts
Sexuality
Material tendencies
The Depths

Middle zone (a, i, u, n, m) :
The personal or empirical Ego with its emotions;
affective tendencies.
Adaptation to the world.
Practical and daily realism.

We therefore apply these ideas not only to the distribution of the writing over the page, but to every graphic entity: address, signature and even to each isolated letter.

Symbolism of the Forms

For example : the *garland*, rounded, open at the top, basin-shaped, can express a nature that is gentle and open to influences coming from *above*. It can also reveal an individual who is notably weak and lacking in backbone. This form however, will never denote intransigence, a disposition to struggle, or toughness.

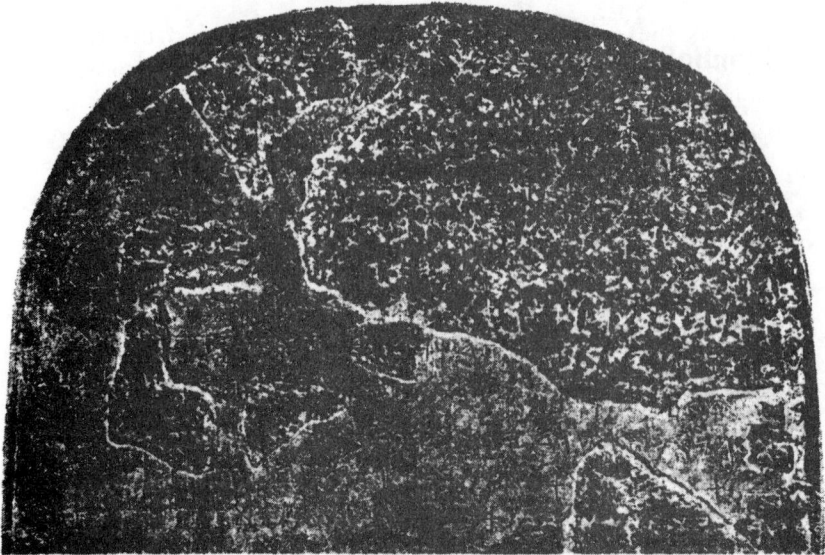

Stone slab inscription of King Mesa, of Moab. The oldest document in the Semite alphabet

Greek writing from books of the 4th Century before our era.

Capital letters of the Middle Ages

It is the *angle* that expresses a trenchant and brusque attitude, stubbornness, or, on the other hand, strength of will and discipline.

The *arcade*, which covers and hides, or which protects, is a sign, that from the start of graphology, has expressed the closed-in, haughty character, protective instincts, or in the case of a writing of superior level, constructiveness.

Ex. 60. - A lunatic's writing. Incoherence in the distribution of the writing. Lack of orientation on the page.

Ex. 61. - A young lunatic's confused and entangled writing.

One is especially struck, here, by the writer's inability to orientate himself within the space of the sheet of paper. The normal individual instinctively has a feeling for the symbolism of space; it is an archetypal notion within him, but the majority of mental lesions are principally characterised in writing by an alteration of this feeling for orientation. Almost all mental patients have a curious way of setting out the writing on the page.

They bunch their writing in each corner of the page, all quite separate from each other, thus symbolising their lack of co-ordination of ideas and their isolation. They may even trace, in two vertical columns, rigid and stereotyped characters (which is, among schizophrenics, a sign of their detachment from their environment).

Thready writing admirably reproduces the behaviour of anxious, ephemeral, indecisive natures, who fly from responsibilities; or who, being intelligent and shrewd, clever and diplomatic, have a fancy for taking the indirect route.

It is in imitating these forms and reliving their symbolism that we can become more aware of their psychological value.

An artificial writing corresponds to a fabricated character, exaggerated size to the desire for, or to feelings of grandeur. Over-developed cross-bars of the capital T or F indicate protection or, when they are placed, high indicate pride or the capacity for leadership, connected writing, indicates the ability to place ideas in sequence.

There even exists, as Pulver has demonstrated, a *projection of the writer's own body image in the writing:* infirmities, the effects of surgical operations, localised maladies, are reflected in the writing. Thus, graphologists have uncovered in twisted or broken lower extensions, the man with a mutilated leg, a clubfoot and certain maladies of the abdominal region (see Duparcy-Jeannez, *Les maladies d'après l'écriture*).

However, while insisting on the symbolic nature of handwriting, one must make an exception for some graphic species that should be considered as a *direct expression of the libido* : pressure, irregularities, tremblings, breaks, ataxia and others. Pressure records, rather than symbolises, the writer's vital energy.

The symbolic value of a handwriting is felt with greater or lesser intensity, not only by specialists, but by all sensitive individuals. Each of us is struck, attracted or repelled, by certain handwritings. This gift, common to all, can be developed. The most gifted pupils whom I trained were on the one hand, painters and sculptors, and, on the other, doctors. The artists sensed the symbolic meaning of a writing line as they would the line of a drawing; while the doctors used their intuition, which had been refined and habituated to combining the meaning of diverse symptoms in order to arrive at an appropriate and exact diagnosis.

The creative act, which consists in sketching a living portrait from the given elements of a writing, can be aroused, can be stimulated, but methods that are too rational or too rigid, kill the creative faculties.

However, one must not lose sight of the fact that spontaneously establishing contact with the hidden meaning of the writing is only the first stage of the graphological task. The true difficulties arise when it comes to producing a full portrait.

Ideographic Conception of Writing

To the symbolism of the writing trail in general, and of each sign in particular, is added *the ideographic conception of writing*. It is universally agreed that our alphabetical writing derives from ideographic writing which evolved over the centuries. The earliest signs represented each object in a more or less simplified form. In some of our letters, one still recognises the primitive image: the capital A, formerly reversed, represented the head of a bull, with horns; the D (the Greek *delta*), typified a door; and the E and the H, in Egyptian writing, was a hieroglyph representing a little man, his arms raised in an attitude of adoration. Our M derives from the broken line that, in hieroglyphic writing, represented water.

We can follow the transformation of the original images from Phoenician writing, with its geometric forms, through the writing of the Greeks and Romans, right up to our printed capitals of today.

The rigid and monumental forms became more flexible during the Middle Ages and developed into the writing we use today. In Greco-Roman writing there was no difference between capitals and small letters; the alphabet was composed solely of forms we preserve today as typographic capitals. This alphabet was modified over the centuries, the forms in use today being fixed with the invention of the printing press. Present day small letters are no more than capitals worn down and slightly modified by use of the goose-quill pen that, toward the end of the Roman Empire, replaced the calamus [1] of the ancients.

---

(1) A pen fashioned from a reed. (Translator's note).

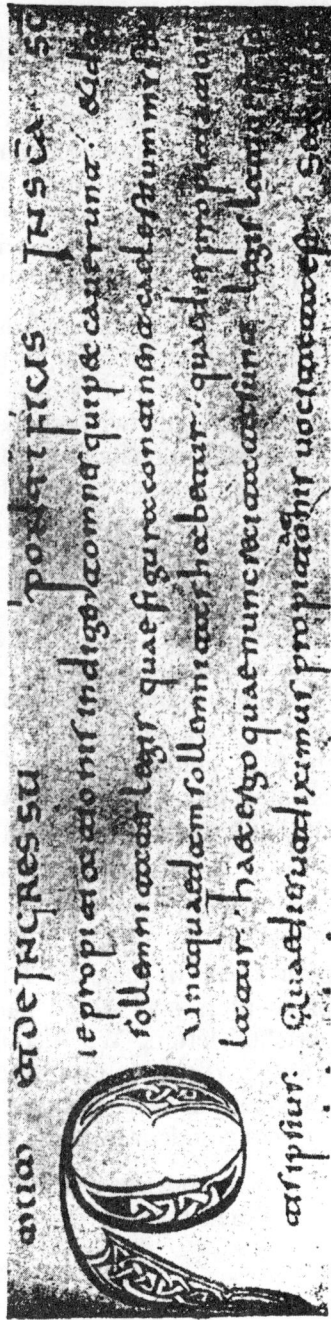

Above : Book writing and handwriting of the 7th and 8th centuries.

Below : Carolingian small letters with an embellished capital letter of the 9th century.

Therefore, there is not any fundamental difference between typeset script and writing done by hand. All these writings have the same origin, Egyptian or Sumerian. In returning to simplified writing, which we call typographic, we go back quite simply to archaic writing. This return to simplification has been seen at various other times in the history of writing: for example, during the Renaissance as well as today, in our attempts at simplification.

The Carolingian small letters, deriving from the Greco-Roman letters, became, in the Middle Ages, Gothic writing, that of the sacred books. We see that Gothic and Latin writing are only two branches derived from the same writing. The Gothic alphabet has tended to disappear and has been replaced, throughout the whole world, even in Germany, by Latin writing, which, with its rounded letters, corresponds much more to the natural movement of life. (We are not speaking here of either the Russian alphabet or the Arabic alphabet).

Handwriting follows faithfully the evolution of all styles through various regions and eras. In the Gothic era, it became long and slender, thus reflecting a spiritual ideal; in the eras smitten by classicism, it became rigid and cold; it became embellished and complicated in the time of the Baroque style.

It is interesting for the graphologist to note that the fancifulness of the capitals was a voluntary creation of the monks of the Middle Ages, who copied the Gospels and pious books by hand and felt the need to mark the beginning of chapters and sacred names by especially enlarged and enriched letters. We therefore see that the capital letters, which particularly express the writer's self-esteem, pride or imagination, have, since their original appearance, served to express grandeur by being distinguished from the others.

Let us come back again to *ideographic writing*. We have established that our current writing undergoes the influence of archetypal imagery such as the symbolism of space. We have seen that, underlying writing, there is an *image*. Thus, it is not surprising that, even in our day, our writing is impregnated by a collective and an individual symbolism. In fact, our writing teems with symbolic representations. Our pursuits, our desires, the images from our unconscious are reflected in it in more or less simplified forms. Graphologists gifted with a special sensitivity have always recognised the meanings of these symbols and amazed the public by their insights.

Schermann, the Viennese clairvoyant graphologist, was famous in his time as a result of his analyses. In truth, he did not create character portraits; he translated into clear language images that appeared to him as alive as in a film. In the figure below, instead of reading the word *Wien* and the

Ex. 62.

Ex. 63. - Handwriting of the aviator, Pégoud.

number II, he saw a steamboat and told the writer: "You desire to take a long sea voyage". This interpretation turned out to be right: the writer had, unwittingly, drawn into his paraph the picture of a boat, the lines of a smokestack, the figure of a prow ploughing the ocean-images that inhabited his unconscious.

The free scriptural movements, as they develop in paraphs, are best suited to reflect our unconscious life. It is easy to recognise, in the aviator, Pégoud's, signature, an aeroplane and the propeller movements.

I have seen the signature of one obsessed by suicide, whose paraph clearly pictured a revolver [1].

Apart from paraphs, a whole primitive ideograph is often hidden in the writing line itself. These observations are interesting, but one should not overestimate their value in graphology. One can be a very good graphologist without having the gift for understanding the meaning of these unconscious representations. They sometimes bring sudden insights, such as the writer's profession or obsessive ideas like those mentioned above, but they are not a sure guide for analysis of the character. The ideographic part of graphology even presents a danger, for one must not lose sight of the fact that all symbolic representations have innumerable meanings that exist on different planes and that the graphologist can be mistaken in choosing an interpretation that is familiar to him, which corresponds to his own psychic being, but not to that of the writer.

A graphologist, for example, discerns in a feminine writing, a clearly designed cross. From this he deduces that the writer had a great sorrow; that, while quite young, she lost a dear one. Big surprise: the interpretation is confirmed as true. I believe that, in this instance, as in many others, it is

---

(1) See the excellent book by Hans Jacoby : *Self-Knowledge through Handwriting*.

a coincidence. The young lady had lost her father, but that cross was not necessarily an expression of her sorrow. For a Catholic graphologist, that sign could only evoke the cross on a tombstone, or the cross as a symbol of suffering. However, it is a symbol much older than Christianity and is not necessarily linked with the tomb or with death. It has many meanings : more particularly, it symbolises perfect balance, the descent of the spirit into matter. A graphologist would be wrong to reduce its meaning to an altogether personal symbolism. I have cited this instance because it is so very characteristic.

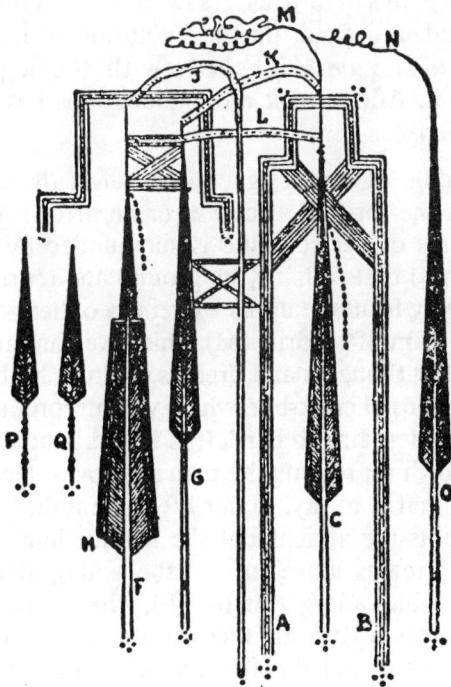

Ex. 64. - A young Jukagire's love letter

Recognition of the symbolic character of handwriting in its entirety, and its transformation into a current language, are more important for the graphologist than the discovery of a few special symbols.

To illustrate this more vividly, I present below a curious example of symbolism. The drawing represents the love letter of a young lady belonging to the tribe of the Jukagires, in eastern Siberia. This graphic expression is not an invention of the young lady, but the current writing of her tribe.

By means of this letter, carved with a knife into a birch bark, the young lady tells her unfaithful lover that she will never be consoled for her loss .

I reproduce this figure as I saw it in an ethnographic exhibition, and in a book on the evolution of handwriting (*Vom Kerbstock zum Alphabet*), with the legend that accompanied it. Added to it are explanations based on the symbolism of space.

In the middle of the design, the young lady represents, herself (C) in the form of a feather or an arrow. A stippled plait informs us of her sex. She is surrounded by a sort of scaffolding (AB) that rests on the ground and represents her house. Emerging from the upper extremity of her person, is a design in the form of tendrils (M) which we can interpret as representing her thoughts and dreams. A little bit below her head, we see a broad cross-bar, which we interpret as crossed arms, a sign of despair. To her left is found another, thinner arrow (G), which represents the man she loves. He is bound to her house, that is to say, to her life, by another cross-bar, which represents the attachment she has for him. The girl's thoughts and dreams move toward the young man. To the latter's left is found a larger arrow (F), which represents the young lady's rival, a Russian, recognisable by her long skirt. She also carries a strippled plait, and one could hardly blame that young girl for having designed her rival's plait shorter than hers.... . Further to the left are found the couple's children, one a little taller than the other. The little family is likewise surrounded by a sort of shorter scaffolding. There must be seen in this effect of perspective the indication that the family is not settled in the same village as the young lady, but is found further away. Outside, and to the right of the main design, we see another arrow, which represents a suitor of the young lady. His thoughts (N) move toward her. By means of this figure, she conveys that another is interested in her, but that she does not respond to his love, for there is no line that binds her to him.

Each line of the design has a meaning. The lines L and K express that close and perfect union that once existed between the girl and the man she loves. But the influence of the more fortunate rival has broken that union, which is expressed by the line J, which comes to separate them.

This letter is completely understandable to the recipient and it can be "read" by all those familiar with the symbolism of space. The writer places to her left everything that belongs to the past: the man she loved and everything concerning him. To her right she inscribes what belongs to the future, the one who, perhaps, will be her husband. In her unconscious, her symbolism corresponds to ours and she places all the spiritual and emotional happenings at the top of her design, while the material things, the house, rest on the ground, pictured here by little cross-shaped dots.

She represents herself with thoughts that, emerging from her head as delicate tendrils, move toward the beloved man and return to her.

The happier Russian girl's thoughts have taken form and become reality. They touch the ground, forming between the two lovers a wall that separates them.

From this primitive representation emanates a very captivating atmosphere. Without knowing it, the writer has described the region where she lives, the clear, cold air, the hard arrows that recall the small, meagre firs of that country's flora. Her whole inner life and its ambience are expressed in the symbolic images of her letter. Could one describe more convincingly and touchingly in words, a situation and a state of mind?

ANALYSIS OF THE HANDWRITING

We have come at this point to the practical part of the work: the application of our knowledge to the analysis of handwritings [1]. To begin with we should become acquainted with a few guidelines.

1. There is no single way, to analyse handwritings; each handwriting inspires within us the procedure to be followed.

2. Every graphologist, during the course of his experience, develops his personal work method, which cannot be imposed on any temperament other than his own.

3. Let us never, though a preconceived idea, look for one psychological type or one complex, but let us be guided solely by the special case we have before us.

4. A signed letter, with its envelope, is the minimum necessary documentation. We must not become seriously involved on the strength of a single writing. As Crépieux-Jamin says, in his *ABC* : "One ought to know, from a

---

(1) These questions have been developed in two printed courses of mine: *Introduction et Perfectionnement de Graphologie Pratique.*

preliminary study of causes, that many people have several handwritings and that the emotional types, particularly, undergo, in the space of hours, constantly renewed impressions. The graphologist, provided with several documents, can determine quite accurately the scope of the writer's impressionability: but, if he has only a few documents, the variability of the writing is a terrible stumbling-block for him. The rule of sufficient documentation has been insisted upon by all the masters of graphology."

5. It is well to bear in mind, as far as possible, the material used (ink, pen, paper). Saudek accords great importance to this matter. For my part, I believe that the writer, in the long run, chooses the materials best suited to rendering the image of the writing he wants to produce.

I would like to draw the attention of graphologists to the following point: in my experience, the broad outlines of a personality: the vital energy, the intelligence, degree of culture, the social level, artistic talents, and superiority or mediocrity, are immediately and unquestionably revealed.

What one discovers about a person after several years of close association, handwriting reveals in a few moments.

This is not the case when it comes to behaviour. To the astonishment of the public, a graphologist will hesitate, or sometimes feel his way, when he is assessing, what we currently call the writer's *character*, that is to say, his manner of being, his reactions as visible to all.

In graphology, therefore, what is produced is the reverse of what we see in everyday life: the main elements, *the synthesis of the personality*, are immediately and rather precisely revealed, while details of little importance, obvious to those within the writer's immediate circle, will only be discovered with the greatest difficulty.

Yet, when one questions the accuracy of a graphological analysis on precisely this point of a writer's behaviour, it is definitely graphology which proves to be right.

Years after an analysis, I have been able to confirm that a handwriting had revealed the deep layers of a character whose behaviour, seemed at the moment of study, to contradict my conclusions. Handwriting records a character's depths and tendencies, but it cannot always show whether these tendencies are being manifested in the present, or whether they exist only in a latent state.

WORK PLAN

Five Stages of the Graphological Analysis

1. *First impression of the writing in its entirety.*

The graphologist must put himself into a receptive state of mind. Participation of the conscious and the unconscious. Discernment of the writer's psychic energy and the writing's general level.

2. *Definition of the writing.*

The graphologist observes both the general effect and the details of the writing. An active and conscious state. He determines the writing's dominant features, then isolates other signs and groups of signs and notes the whole. He checks, from the general list of the species, whether he has overlooked any of them.

3. *Interpretation of the signs.*

The graphologist gives to each graphic symbol (sign or group of signs) its psychological equivalent. (See the *Dictionary*).

The psychological components are arranged in accordance with how they relate to one another (signs that are predominant, confirmatory, complementary, com-pensatory, contradictory).

4. *Second part of the interpretation*

Use the *question-naire*. The writer is classified according to the typologies (attitudes and functions).

5. *The synthesis*.

Construction of the writer's portrait.

Let us go back again to these successive stages.

1 - *First impression of the writings in its entirety.*

It is imperative always to start with the general impression and never to lose sight of its general effect when noting down the signs and the interpretations which follow them.

During the first stage, it is necessary to put oneself in a state of complete receptivity in order to receive from a writing the first impression which is, in large part, an unconscious one.

Subsequently, it will be become more and more conscious through investigation of the details.

It is during the course of this passive contemplation that the graphologist receives the impression of the writing's *general level*, of what Crépieux-Jamin calls the *harmony*, Klages, the *Formniwo*, and Pulver, *the very essence of the individual*. In order to learn to recognise a writing's value, the novice graphologist has only to compare a certain number of documents coming from different writers. The impression of the superiority of one writing over another becomes clear very quickly. I have conducted this experiment with many graphologists, colleagues, beginners or amateurs. With the exception of a few nuances of interpretation, all are in agreement. Exceptional intuition is not necessary for assessing an individual's value from his writing. Graphological experience helps to develop this sensitivity.

Each sign, as we will see later, *is invested with its particular nuance according to the writing's general level* (see pp.229)..

The level of the writing does not depend on one quality alone. Writings that are small, or large, pasty, or fine, can all have a good general level. However, certain graphic qualities largely determine the level : the rhythm, the combinations and the unaffected but natural originality of the forms. All exaggeration, and this is true for all the species, militates against a good general level.

2 and 3 - Definition of the writing and the interpretation of the signs

Let us go back again to Crépieux-Jamin's *ABC* : "In order to define a writing, one must seek to relive the movements of the person who traced them. To this end, one imitates these movements in the air with the hand, to stimulate the imagination. One examines it at a distance of about sixty centimetres, thus favouring observation of the writing's large movements thereby provisionally eliminating the less exteriorised movements.
One considers it several times, for one or two seconds only, noting each time "what one has seen".

It should be added that a magnifying glass is always very useful. By isolating certain parts of the writing in order to observe them with the magnifying glass, one becomes aware of many of the details (little pauses, joinings, etc.), that escape the naked eye.

For the experienced graphologist, definition and interpretation become superimposed. He cannot refrain from immediately feeling the psychological value of a graphic sign, but he will do well, while still noting his impressions, to continue a definition of a purely descriptive kind.

The beginner, however, will benefit from clearly distinguishing the different stages. The definition should be completely established before beginning the interpretation.

The general level having been determined as in 1., we must now investigate first whether the writing is :

- organised, unorganised or disorganised,
- harmonious or inharmonious,
- regular or irregular.

Having determined these broad outlines, which already furnish a framework for the other signs, we isolate the dominant features from the whole (on average from 6 to 12) - that is to say, those signs that give to the writing its special character, for example : writing that is rounded, pasty, large, right-slanted, etc.

Finally, we isolate the less decisive signs that are grouped around the dominant features.

We check, according to the general list of species, whether any have been overlooked.

The definition having being thus established, we attribute to each graphic sign its psychological equivalent.

The experienced graphologist has his dictionary of interpretations in his head. The one offered at the end of this work can serve as an aide memoire or as a stimulus. He will add to it from the results of his own experience. The beginner will benefit from using the dictionary regularly.

It is not only a question of choosing among several interpretations the one that agrees best with the writing that is being analysed, but of modifying it if necessary.

The signs can be :

- predominant
- complementary
- confirmatory
- compensatory
- contradictory

It is a question of uncovering the interplay of the signs and of evaluating the role of each. The art of the graphologist consists precisely in attributing to each sign its relative value.

The graphological analysis is a work of observation, of combination and deductions. One should never make use of a psychological combination or deduction without verifying whether the writing truly contains the signs that correspond to what one has deduced, for it is the graphic signs that underpin the psychological combinations.

4 - Second part of the interpretation

Consult the *questionnaire*. The writer is classified according to the typologies (attitudes and functions). The technical terms: introversion, extraversion, libido, complexes, etc., are to be avoided. In the portrait, *one describes the writer*, striving above all to be understandable, lively and natural.

5 - The synthesis

The difficulties of graphological analysis are not of a graphic kind. They reside in the psychological synthesis and in the presentation of the portrait. It is relatively easy to establish a few general lines of a character: it is infinitely more difficult to paint a life-like portrait.

The beginner should confine himself to making brief and pertinent analyses and to essential remarks about which he is sure, rather then trying to inflate the portrait with more or less fanciful details.

The graphological portrait can be seen from different angles and it is the writing itself which will suggest to the graphologist which one is most suitable. How the portrait is structured depends on the purpose for which it is intended.

In the outlines demanded by company bosses, one mentions in particular the qualities and aptitudes suitable to the profession (see the second part of the *questionnaire*).

For professional guidance of the young, the analysis should be more extensive and also more in-depth.

In *comparative analyses* (marriages, partnerships) the particular guiding factors are two attitudes and the four functions; one will look for complementary qualities in the future partners. (First and second part of the *questionnaire*).

Finally, *the complete analysis* should answer all the points in the *questionnaire*.

In the study of a writing, one can look at it from different points of view, for example:

- Predominance of the male or female side: problems that arise from it and their possible solutions.

- Predominance of the extraverted or introverted attitude. Indication of the dominant functions and the functions which need to be developed.

- The *Persona* or *the private individual*. Harmony or lack of harmony between the different layers of the psyche, between the writer's behaviour and his true nature.

- *Innate gifts* : Their realisation or non-realisation.

In any case, it is important *to establish a plan* for the elaboration of the portrait. More often than not, it is the writing itself that will dictate this, whether on the one hand, the writer can be fathomed only bit by bit, or whether, on the other, his whole personality is evident from the beginning.

In general, I recommend that a subject should never be left feeling discouraged. After having indicated the weaknesses to be combated, the graphologist should bring together, at the conclusion of the portrait, all the positive elements of the writer's nature so as to help the latter to find his true way. Our role is to enlighten those who come to us and not to dishearten them.

* * *

So that the reader can verify the analyses, I have chosen as examples two handwritings of known personalities.

The objection can be raised that one is influenced by what one already knows about the writers. My reply to this is that I have strictly used for the definition and the interpretation, only the signs contained in the *dictionary*. It is in the synthesis alone that I mention what everyone knows about the writer of the first document: that is to say, that Yvette Guilbert was a great artist; the same applies to the writing of Trarieux d'Egmont, a writer and astrologist of my acquaintance.

QUESTIONNAIRE

The writer's vital energy?

Intensity of the libido?

Direction of the libido? Extraversion or introversion: that is to say, predominance of the outer or inner life.

Psychic functions?
(Thinking, Feeling, Sensation, Intuition).

- Principal function (rational or irrational) and the auxiliary functions.

- Interplay of the functions according to the tables in the corresponding chapter.

- Is one function developed to the detriment of the others?

Strength and role of the *Will?*

Strength and role of *Sensuality?*

Relations between the conscious and the unconscious elements?

Inner resistances, ambivalence, problems?

In the event of inner conflict, what is its source?

Is there a complex? Repression? Compensation? Over-compensation? Of what kind?

Nervous condition of the writer?

Does he belong to the cyclothyme or the schizothyme type? Expanded or contracted?

Is the character virile or effeminate?

Aptitudes and Behaviour

Intelligence (logic, association of ideas, judgement, originality of thought, assimilative or creative faculties).

Imagination, artistic or literary talents.

Eloquence Sensitivity.

Concentration.

Order, method.

Faculty for adaptation, foresight.

Organisational ability.

Practical sense, ingenuity.

Initiative.

Combative energy or stamina for the "long haul".

Work efficiency, activity, application.

Independence.

Aptitude for leadership.

Openness or concealment.

Psychological sense.

Devotion.

Sociability.

Discretion.

Diplomacy.

Loyalty, honesty.

Many of these questions were answered on determining the attitude type and the function type, but it is always useful to study a human being from several angles and try to acquaint oneself with all the aspects of his nature.

One will then be able to ask whether the writer is [1]:

Careless or conscientious.

Stubborn or quickly discouraged.

Impulsive or circumspect.

Decisive or indecisive.

Distrustful or trustful.

Tolerant or intolerant.

Anxious and uneasy or carefree.

Constant or inconstant.

Gullible or sceptical.

With quick or slow understanding.

Autonomous in his opinions or inclined to repeat the opinions or others.

Talkative or uncommunicative.

Clear-minded or confused.

Ambitious or self-effacing.

Vain or modest.

Selfish or unselfish.

Stingy, economical, generous or spendthrift.

Authoritarian or liberal.

Hard or tender.

---

(1) As per the statistical inquiry questionnaire of G.Heymans and E. Wiersma. (René Le Senne, *Traité de Caractèrologie*. Presses Universitaires, 1945).

GRAPHOLOGICAL PORTRAITS
Two examples of analyses

Yvette Guilbert (76 years of age)

I. - First sight of the writing's general effect

General impression : good level. Strong libido. Considerable vital impulse in view of the writer's age.

II. - Definition of the writing

Signs to be considered in the first place :

   a) The writing is organised, with signs of disorganisation

   b) Irregular

   c) Rhythmic (with some irregularities in the rhythm).

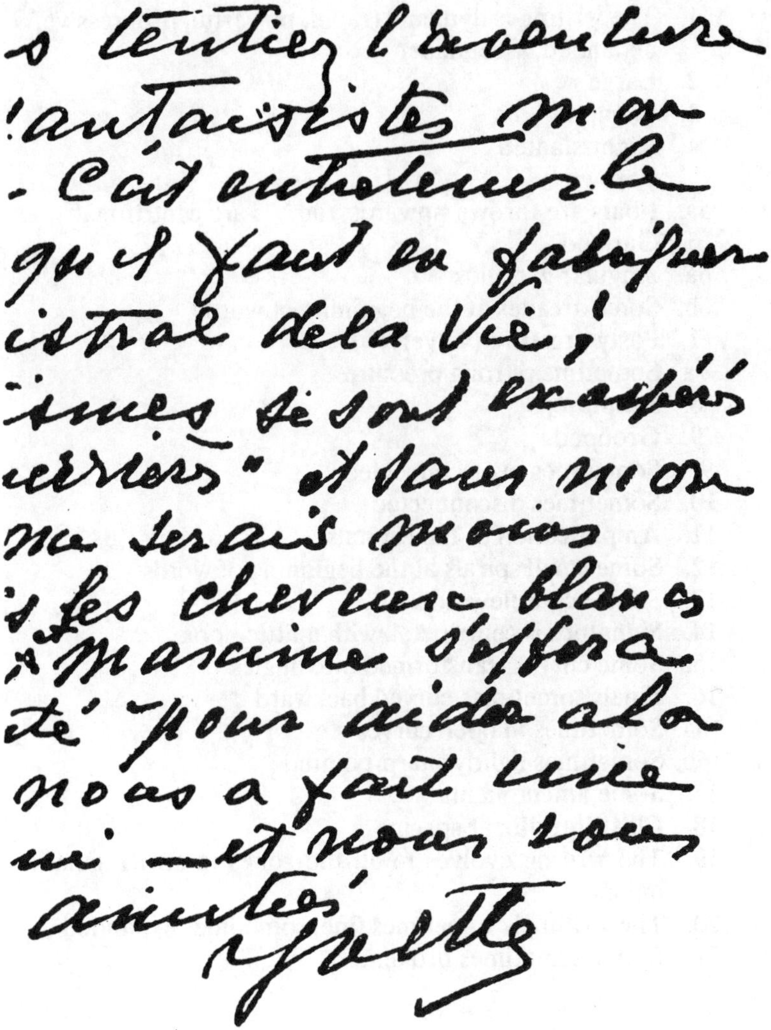

Ex. 65. - Yvette Guilbert's writing.

Dominant features and other signs :

1. The writing is dynamic (rapid, powerful, progressive, expanded, ascendant)
2. Large
3. Precipitated
4. Right-slanted
5. Thrown
5a. t-bars are thrown upwards, the V's are centrifugal
6. Garlands
6a. Angular garlands
6b. Some arcades at the beginning of words
7. Pasty pressure (velvety)
7a Sometimes strong pressure
8. Simplified
9. Grouped
9a. Sometimes over-connected
10. Sometimes disconnected
11. Amplification of the capitals
12. Some small spirals at the beginning of words
13. Some superelevations
14. Signature is centripetal, with a little hook
15. Some curves transformed into angles
16. Finals sometimes curved backward
16a. Sometimes in open curves
16b. Sometimes lightly sharp-pointed
17. Some amendments
18. Clear interlinear spacing
19. The writing evolves in all the zones in an irregular manner
20. The writing is sometimes fine, sometimes expanded
21. Letter sometimes broken.

III. - *Interpretation of the writing*

Great intensity of life. Strong libido.

a) No hindrances in the writing act

b) Great emotivity. Impressionability

c) Depth of soul, originality. Vigorous temperament

*Interpretation of the graphic Signs
enumerated above : (1 to 21)*

1. *Strong libido, in progression.*

   Powerful vital impulse. Psychic energy that is freely discharged. Intense activity, euphoria, love of life. Good health. Fast thinking, impatience, persuasiveness, enthusiasm, communicative nature. Generosity.

2. *Strong libido, in progression. Extraversion. Feeling and Sensation type.*

   Self-esteem, pride, euphoria, enthusiasm, activity, imagination, intuition.

3. *Libido in progression, extraversion. Intuition.*

   Lively mind, great activity, lack of prudence, impatience, agitation; simple and natural behaviour.

4. Extraversion, Feeling type. Activity. The affective tendencies take precedence over the reasoning faculty. Ardour.

5. Impulsiveness, spontaneity, effusion, exuberance, exaggeration, dominating disposition. Will.

5a. Mystical tendencies, spiritual aspirations

6. Extraversion. Feeling type. Receptivity, attachment. Contact with others.

6a. Firmness, tenacity. Stubbornness.

6b. Pride, artistic sense.

7. *Sensation.* Sensuality, plastic arts, artistic sense.

7a. Energy, perseverance.

8. Superior intelligence. Introversion. Thinking and Intuition, culture, activity. The writer aims at the essential.

9. *Libido in progression.* - Continuity of thought and effort. Logic, intelligence.

9a. Stubbornness in ideas. Cyclothymic type

10. *Intuition.* Associative and irrational ideas.

11. Imagination, illusions, self-esteem. Tendency to exaggeration. Varied interests of an intellectual and practical kind.

12. A bit of diplomacy, a bit of "slyness", coquetry.

13. Inferiority complex over-compensated by pride.

14. The need to be precise. Energy. Monopolising tendencies.

15. Tendency to harshness and stubbornness.

16. Desire to seduce.

16a. Amiability.

16b. Critical sense and aggressivity.

17. Self-observation. Desire to do well.

18. Mental clarity and fluency of speech.

19. Richness of personality, variety of interests, emotivity.

20. Intellectual and artistic interests.

21. Fatigue. Age becoming a factor despite extraordinary youthfulness of character.

The psychological components are set out in relation to one another.

Evaluation of the Libido

Its Intensity

1. Strong libido, in progression
2. Strong libido, in progression
3. Libido in progression
7. Strong libido
8. Libido in progression
9. Libido in progression

Its Direction

2. Extraversion
4. Extraversion
6. Extraversion
8. Introversion

Relation of the Functions to one another

2. Feeling and Sensation type
3. Intuition
4. Feeling type
5. Intuition
6. Feeling type
7. Sensation
8. Thinking and Intuition type
10. Intuition type

In this extraordinary individual, all the functions are well developed. However, there is a clear preponderance of *Feeling*. This is indicated as a result of the interpretation of all the graphic signs. Intuition is the auxiliary function,

Sensation a complementary function. Thinking, the least developed function, serves as a check, as a counterweight. Feeling, the principal function, is directed outward: Thinking, the least developed function, is directed inward.

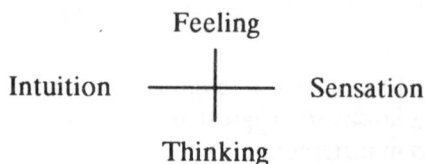

Feeling

Intuition ———+——— Sensation

Thinking

IV. - Answers to the questionnaire

- I -

The writer's *will* is firm, consciously goal-directed. Sensuality is developed without drawing all the libido to it. The conscious and unconscious elements are in harmony and come together in the domain of creation. There is no discordant "tug-of-war" and little repression. The rational and irrational elements are well balanced.

The inferiority complex is compensated by work, happy contact with others and the self-fulfilment the writer finds in artistic creation. As the libido is in a state of progression, the complex is resolved. Perhaps it has served its purpose as a point of departure.

The nervous condition denotes: excitement, over-activity, exaltation.

Cyclothymic type, but not in its pure state. Feminine character, with masculine elements: will, intellect, activity.

Superior intelligence, lively mind. Overflowing, creative imagination. Independence, but great sentimental attachment. Initiative.

- II -

Combative energy and staying power.

Good working ability but unevenness of attention.

Tendency to dissipation, generally controlled.

Little order.

Flexibility.

Social sense.

Good contact with others.

Average organisation.

Developed practical sense.

Frankness touched with a bit of feminine diplomacy.

Loyalty.

Sincerity and honesty

V. - The Portrait

The writing strikes one with the power of its vitality, the richness of its varied elements, by its extraordinary dynamism.

The writer has a generous, exuberant nature. Carried away by the irresistible impetuosity of her temperament, she communicates her enthusiasm to others, enriches and inspires those around her.

Brimming with vitality and gifted, at the same time, with a refined intelligence, she is the born artist. In her, heart and intuition, intelligence and practical sense harmonise in a rare union, but it is the heart that rules. Intellect follows in the wake of feeling.

The writer drinks fully from the depths of her soul, with the freedom of a child. From this comes her inspiration, the plasticity of her creation, which is a dream come to life again. Her passionate and ardent feelings evolve not only in the sphere of personal relations, but on all planes - she would like to embrace everything. In her, the lovers of every age live anew; she sheds all their tears, vibrates with all their feelings and that warmth embraces the public, whom she moves and uplifts. Communion, union in ecstasy; that is her secret.

All her talents, all her capacities serve her in the achievement of her supreme goal : creation in love.

Even her weaknesses are simply obstacles that stimulate her powers: any feelings of weakness and she galvanises herself so as to overcome the difficulty, to surpass herself.

Her tenacious will carries her over bouts of fatigue, inevitable defeats, nervous depression and momentary discouragement, pushing her ever onward.

Receptive, infinitely feminine in the domain of the heart, she calls upon a masculine firmness and energy when it comes to achieving her inspiration, to expressing the richness of her nature in artistic activity.

The writer is strong-minded, not a compromiser. She is not conciliatory and can be abrupt with people, but she is never spiteful. Smiling, she uses feminine wiles, should it seem opportune, with a mischievous and mocking air.

Her sense of values, her critical mind are not of the destructive sort. Her good sense, her practical mind are in her case factors of order: self-observation, far from being unhealthy, serves her as an instrument of control.

Her stubbornness, likewise, is a necessary element for succeeding in her goals. She rebels against everything that could stifle her spirit; against prejudices, oppressive customs, narrowness, stupidity. She rebels, or even goes beyond that, and the gods have favoured her with that rare and superior gift: humour.

The writer is at times aggressive, harsh, impatient, nervous, but never vulgar. She is proud, ambitious, without ever being pompous.

She is a force of nature, a source of overflowing life, who nevertheless accepts the control of the intellect.

* * *

Gabriel Trarieux d'Egmont,
an elderly Frenchman

I. - First sight of the writing's general effect

General impression : High level of personality, good education, broad culture. Strong libido.

II. - Definition of the writing

Signs to be considered first of all :
1. The writing is organised
2. Slightly irregular
3. Harmonious

Dominant features and other signs :
4. Good layout
5. Disconnected writing
5a. Writing sometimes connected (grouped)
6. Vertical, or
6a. Slightly right-slanted
7. Sometimes semi-angular
7a. Sometimes semi-rounded
7b. Sometimes semi-arcadic
8. Slightly rigid
8a. Some stylisation
9. Simplified
10. Sober
10a. Some enlarged capitals

Chère Madame. Je vous envoie ci-joint votre horoscope.
J'espère qu'il vous intéressera. Il est sujet à une réserve que
vous connaissez : l'heure exacte. L'analyse des chiffres vous
sous vous permettra de la vérifier, de la corriger, au besoin. Ce
travail n'est qu'un point de départ. Vous devez le compléter
par vous-même

J'ai gardé le meilleur souvenir de nos brèves et ré-
centes causeries. Je regrette qu'elles soient terminées. Je
vous prie d'agréer mes meilleurs hommages, et tous mes
voeux pour l'année qui s'ouvre.

Gabriel Trarieux d'Egmont

Ex. 66. – Gabriel Trarieux d'Egmont's writing.

11.   Signature larger and more important than the text

12.   Precise pressure

12a.   Pasty in places

13.   Left margin a bit irregular

14.   Right margin regular

15.   Clear interlinear spacing

15a.   Parallel lines

15b.   Rising lines

16.   Normal spaces between words

17.   Writing is poised

18.   Slight preponderance of the lower zone over the upper zone (the M's and s's prolonged downwards)

18a.   Some superelevations

19.   Inflated ovals

20.   Simplified, "l's" and "t's" in the form of sticks

21.   Sharp-pointed finals

22.   The "J" is amplified at its base

23.   Inhibition at the beginning of the "J"

24.   Lower extensions often open

25.   The "t" of "travail" (5th line) is tremulous, angular

26.   The t-bars are short and sharp-pointed

27.   Closed "a's" and "o's"

28.   Writing is neat

29.   Signature is rising, enriched, ending in an energetic downward paraph

29a.   Thrown t-bars

29b.   The Christian name is larger than the surname.

29c.   Spiral at the beginning of the Christian name.

III. - Interpretation of the above signs

Superior general level, remarkable personality, broad culture, high social level. Intensity of life.

1. No impediments of a material kind.
2. Emotivity, sensibility, imagination, impressionability.
3. Depth of soul.
4. Taste, culture.
5. *Introversion, Intuition*, spontaneous, irrational formation of ideas.
5a. Sequence of ideas, intelligent realisation.
6. Firmness, reserve, pride, lack of spontaneity, mistrust, egoism.
6a. Interest in others.
7. Firmness, tenacity, intransigence, lack of flexibility in behaviour.
7a. *Thinking Type.* Receptivity, supple intelligence.
7b. Reserve, distant pride, discretion. *Introversion.* Intense, but hidden, inner life. Reserve, repression, precision, severity. Emotivity hidden behind an impenetrable Persona.
8a. Contraction, sense of form, egocentricity.
9. *Introversion, Thinking and Intuition types.* Superior intelligence, culture, activity.
10. *Introversion. Thinking.* Moderation, reflection, modest, prudent, orderly, methodical. Coldness of heart.
10a. Imagination. Illusion.

11. Overcompensated inferiority complex.

12. Strong libido. *Thinking Type.* Delicate health, but resistant. Moderate energy. Perseverance. Precise mind, orderly and clear. Self-control. Objectivity. Dryness of heart.

12a. Love of life. Moderate sensuality.

13. Emotivity.

14. Good organisation of time and money.

15. Mental clarity.

15a. Sense of duty, self-control.

15b. Enthusiasm.

16. Clarity.

17. Moderation, calmness, reflective mind, prudence, self-control.

18. Instinctive, materialistic tendencies.

18a. Interests of an intellectual and spiritual nature.

19. Vanity, egocentricity.

20. Objectivity.

21. Critical sense. Aggressiveness, combativeness.

22. Vanity, self-esteem..

23. Hesitation, prudence.

24. Independence, non-attachment, indifference to sexual life.

25. Slight disorganisation.

26. Criticism. Irony. Conflict in the intellectual domain.

27. Closed-in character.

28. Meticulous, orderly mind.

29. The signature : Vital spirit. Fighting spirit.

   a) High aspirations.
   b) Ambition and self-esteem.
   c) Egocentricity.

The Psychological Components
are set in relation to one another

Type of attitude

   5. Introversion
   7b. Introversion
   9. Introversion
   10. Introversion

Function Type

   5. Intuition type
   7a. Thinking type
   9. Thinking and Intuition type
   10. Thinking type
   12. Thinking type, Intuition

We have from the above, a picture of an *introverted type* with few extraverted tendencies.

According to the results of the analysis, the writer is a *Thinking* type, with auxiliary function *Intuition*. It is Feeling that is the inferior function and not Sensation, since we found in (12a) and in (18) material and instinctive tendencies, whereas the inferiority of the Feeling function is confirmed by points (10) and (12).

All the psychological qualities determined from the different graphic species are in agreement. There are only six qualities that are apparently contradictory to the rest of the analysis.

Let us analyse these qualities to see if they are truly opposed to the psychological type we have determined up to this point :

- Activity

- Modesty

- Illusions

- Enthusiasm

- Instinctive, material tendencies

- Combativeness

Activity - corresponds to the intensity of life as verified in the writer. One should not believe that introverts are inactive individuals absorbed in retrospection (a very widespread error). There exists in all normal individuals a need to act, at least in certain areas. In a thinker like Trarieux d'Egmont, activity will be deployed especially in the realm of the intellect.

Modesty - is explained by the writer's good education and cultivated taste, which compensate his pride. Introverts are often modest and reserved in their behaviour while still having a very lively feeling about their own value.

Illusions - are common to all men, even the most objective. Introverted intuition inclines to the irrational, to reveries in solitude. The intuitive thinker recognises, perhaps, the illusory character of certain of his ideas, without being able to, or without wanting to give them up.

Enthusiasm - is a quality that is frequent in individuals endowed with intuition and who live through their aspirations and hopes. Elan, in this writer, is particularly shown in the spiritual realm and is related to his work.

Instinctive, material tendencies - are only the manifestations of the instinct for self-preservation.

His *combativeness* is likewise shown on the level of ideas.
Aggressive extraversion is not rare in introverts. It is the
counterpart of their withdrawn and distant attitude. If the
introvert exteriorises, he can easily go beyond the limits of
moderation, to the amazement of the extraverted type.
Exteriorisation however, wearies and enervates him and he
withdraws all the more willingly into his innermost being.

All the signs in the analysis complement and confirm each
other, to sketch a character with a rare unity of tendencies.
Even the apparent contradictions are essential to the shaping
of a living whole.

IV. - Answers to the questionnaire

- I -

Strong libido : introverted type.

Function type : Thinking - Intuition.

Thinking is developed to the detriment of Feeling, which
is why an impression of coldness emanates from the writing.
Neither Thinking nor Intuition give to the individual the
warmth that Feeling and Sensation can produce.

The writer's *will* is strong and firm, directed toward a
goal: the achievement of his work, his self-control.

Sexuality is partly repressed, partly sublimated.

Conscious elements prevail in his psyche. There is tense-
ness of the conscious. The latter partly stifles the unconscious tendencies, unless he uses them toward a well-
defined goal.

There is inner conflict, ambivalence.

The writer is primarily *rational* (Thinking being a rational function), with intuitive, irrational inspiration.

The writer has *an inferiority complex over-compensated in pride.*

Nervous state : vibrant sensitivity, irritability, partly controlled.

Schizothymic, retracted type.

A virile character.

- II -

Superior intelligence. Assimilative and creative faculties.

Often a sectarian spirit, for Feeling is not there to render intellectual judgement flexible.

Rich imagination, artistic and literary talents.

Great independence.

Initiative that is set in motion slowly, after hesitations.

Energy, especially in the long term.

Great working abilities.

Extraordinary concentration.

The writer loves order, to the point of being meticulous and crotchety.

Difficult adaptation, little flexibility in his behaviour.

Social sense is more theoretical than practical.

Contact is difficult.

Exclusive in his relationships.

Good organisation of time and money.

Psychological awareness and understanding of others remain on a theoretical level.

Little spontaneity, but an upright, honest and loyal character.

Disdains the beaten track. Lives in conformity with his principles.

V. - The Portrait

The writing reveals a remarkable man, of superior intelligence and extensive culture.

The writer is a profound thinker, withdrawn, closely concerned with his work. His lucid thinking dominates everything; it is precise, flexible, logical, subtle and penetrating. He is able to see things from several angles.

The writer also has the gift of intuition : that spontaneous vision that surpasses the limits of reason, to understand and to create.

It is that union of objective thinking and inspiration, of the scientific and the irrational vision that bestows on the writer his wholly original mark.

He gives himself entirely to his work, living in the world of ideas. The future, with all its possibilities, stimulates his intuition, evokes his intellectual curiosity, carries him beyond the present moment. In all things, he sees "the future".

Passionately interested in scientific research and pushed ever further by his intuition, he is an astrologer and writer. He wants to prove by logic what came to him by the least rational means.

This cast of mind, this loftiness, does not render life easy, either on the practical level or on the level of feeling. It is particularly in the domain of human feelings that one sees a weakness in him.

Orientated towards the invisible, he neglects human contacts; he is cold, inaccessible, often ignoring what is going on around him.

He shocks his immediate circle with his intransigence, his severity, his aloof pride and lack of adaptation to other people's rhythm of life. The others, for their part, are often unaware that, behind the impenetrable facade and the calmness acquired by constant self-control, there is hidden an almost painful sensibility, an excessive emotivity.

His apparent coldness is often nothing more than an awkward defence of a nervous and impressionable individual who fears the knocks and conflicts of life. The writer rarely exteriorises and is appalled by any showy manifestation on the part of others. Thus, a void has been created around him, a solitude that causes him suffering in moments of weakness.

However, when he plunges into his work, he forgets everything. Swept away by his enthusiasm, intoxicated by his vision and the process of creation, he tries to render accessible to others and to perpetuate in his work, his inner world peopled by images.

He is egoistic and egocentric, but, is not the man who creates compelled to defend himself, to defend his sanctuary against any profane intrusion? The writer's ambition goes much further than a commonplace ambition of a social kind; it aspires to other horizons.

His loyalty, his integrity are in no doubt. The writer scorns the beaten track and although withdrawn, he is honest and sincere. His sense of duty is very strongly developed; he lives in conformity with his principles.

With his methodical and orderly mind, he is obsessively conscientious and meticulous. Never satisfied with his research, with his studies, he takes exactness to the limit.

Sometimes, he also loses himself in details.

He is a great worker, tireless, always in search of the truth. His very marked critical sense can be aggressive and take the form of hurtful irony.

The writer knows his worth, and does not fail to make his superiority felt by others. The exaggerated self-esteem he hides beneath the modesty of a man who has been well brought up and has good taste, makes one suspect an underlying inferiority feeling. Could it be that the writer is so sure of himself because really, at, heart he harbours doubts about himself?

This seeker has detached himself from life and its pleasures, but he has nevertheless remained sensitive in some respects. He loves beauty, a carefully fostered atmosphere, good food, friendly "get-togethers" where he feels he is understood. However, the true ties that join him to his fellows are spiritual ones.

He is a fighter who defends *his ideas* against everything and everyone. A man who, in spite of delicate health and advanced age, has maintained an intensity of life, an extraordinary courage and idealism.

* * *

There are of necessity numerous repetitions in setting out the formal procedure of these two analyses. In practice, the stages are subsumed into a global perspective that rises above details.

In order to preserve, in the development of the portrait, the freshness of the first vision, one must forget the successive stages and re-live the writing's movements. But the fact of having determined all the details saves one from going astray when, afterwards, one gives free rein to intuition.

Jean Cocteau [1]

Jean Cocteau's handwriting brings us face to face with the most troublesome problems. Not only does he transgress all the boundaries between handwriting and drawing, but he reverses everything that seems to have been learnt in graphology, while yet admitting, himself, the profound truth of the latter.

Cocteau's handwriting is not lovely - except in a few scattered letters - it is not harmonious; it is disorderly, filiform, very irregular; it defies all our laws - yet it is infinitely expressive.

It is impossible for the graphologist to forget Jean Cocteau's personality. Knowing, as we do, who he is, what he does, what he creates, we are now going to try to understand him, to rediscover him through his writing.

Where is the key that will open for us the mysterious domain of this soul, this tight rope walker who does a balancing act in both the infernal and celestial worlds and plays battledore and shuttlecock with the invisible, in the manner of children? I believe quite simply that Cocteau has remained a child. The first characteristic of his handwriting is its *childishness*.

It reflects not the well brought up child, shaped by adult values, but the child as seen by Freud: endowed with polymorphous eroticism, with insatiable curiosity, a cruel, truthful child, without consideration or shame, possessive, egocentric, bi-sexual, full of an animal grace, amoral, for he lives outside man's laws.

Even more than this, he is a creative child, whose spontaneous drawings are like those of the tiny tots seen in

---

(1) The letter is part of the collection *Les Nouvelles Epitres*, published by the Monde Illustré, Paris.

modern schools - an imaginative, ingenious child who moves about his kingdom, from which he has not yet been driven.

Cocteau has resisted levelling influences, rebelling against boredom and conventions; he has remained very close to his Angelic-Demonic brethren; he has not consented to become a man.

Very often in his work, he insists on the fundamental, ineluctable difference between the poet and the "adjusted" man. His handwriting illustrates that difference. It abounds in unconstraint, disorder, dream, "magical electricity". Cocteau hears the voices of silence, which are nothing less than inspiration from afar.

Call it a neurosis but we should also understand that only a single aspect of this complex being has been touched upon. Let us try to see him from an angle that comes closer to the perceptions of the divine eye than the medical eye.

Cocteau's drawing is traced with a pen; it continues the writing. The lower extension of "Je" completes the drawings. Thus, starting up from the unconscious depths which know no limits, a surge of energy embraces a whole enchanting world whose door the poet alone knows how to open and close.

ce qui m'importe, c'est
l'aspect d'une lettre
Car c'est à cet aspect qu'un
graphologue nous déconne
mieux que d'après notre style.

Je donne ajoute à cette vie intérieure
qu'une lettre doit communiquer à son
lecteur

Voyez l'champagne le "Nouvelles Epoque"
... m'a ... une lettre . puis-je ce à

Ex. 67. - Jean Cocteau.

à collection, je me laisse prendre à ce terme.
n'importe quoi, à travailler avec vous, à
huiler avec le dé... d'une âme inconnue.

Rien ne dégage plus cette électricité mirage
d'un bavardage entre personnes qui s'entendent à
demi-mot, que le genre épistolaire

Lorsque ..., en somme, ne reçoivent que des lettres? deux
... envie appelé, des signes de souffrance. S'ils répondent
ils reçoivent ... joie à leur réponse... qui exige une
... Hélas les lettres sont innombrables. Chacun voit
... le seul à nous écrire. Que faire! Le artiste

Ex. 67b. – Jean Cocteau's writing

Ex. 68. - Renoir

A curious enigma, Renoir's writing : nothing in these precise, thrown strokes evokes here the painter of the rose-tinted flesh of the *Women Bathers*, of the enchanting sun of the Midi. One would believe one was encountering a pure intellectual or scientist, an art critic, rather than the evocative portrayer of innocent, simple life, untroubled by the intellect.

Such a handwriting is a terrible stumbling-block for the graphologist and only the most painstaking work, reaching down to the very deepest springs of creation, could come close to its secret.

For Renoir, the impressions of reality, absorbed by the most refined senses, seem to pass through the filter of a pitilessly lucid mind, before finding their definitive expression in an immortal creation.

Ex. 69. - A. Sisley

There exists a slight resemblance between Renoir's handwriting and that of Sisley. Rapid, clear simple, spontaneous, their writing unfolds freely, with an élan and confidence that reveals the highly gifted being.

But Sisley has a more impatient, more impassioned, more impetuous temperament. His strong, thrown strokes are formidable weapons of attack.

Ex. 70. - Pissaro

The handwriting of a painter who is a painter above all else. Large, slightly pasty, velvety, soft, passionate and sensual, it recalls the paint brush more than the pen. The avid, insatiable receptivity to the innumerable impressions that the life of forms and colours offer, is stronger than any power of reflection. And love! There is the spontaneous gift of the creative man to the inexhaustible forces of Mother Nature, the mysterious union with everything that lives.

This document dates from the period when Pissaro had not yet come under Cezanne's influence, which, as time went on, was to render his art more subtle. He was still the painter who "wields the paint", as his writing reveals.

PART THREE

Foreword

Graphic signs are the symbolic expression of the libido, as it was defined in the foregoing chapters. Alone or in groups, they reflect the inexhaustible variety inherent in that energy.

The framework of our graphology is thus rather extensible in order to allow room for the limitless possibilities in the blending of signs.

I have held as closely as possible to the definitions of Crépieux-Jamin and his school. To his interpretations I have added those of Pulver, Klages, Saudek and my own.

The libido, protean-like in its essence, may be expressed in physical and psychic symptoms. These two aspects of the libido, then, will often be found in the following tables. The reader will see that the Jaminian definitions will tend to express the derived tendencies, as well as the talents, abilities and behaviour, while my interpretations try to touch the deeper psychic layers, the essentially primitive tendencies. It is for that reason that, in the following table, I have placed my interpretations in the first position.

In no way do I claim to be complete. To the present dictionary can be added all further observations and discoveries.

Opposite each sign is listed a range of possible interpretations. The whole art of the graphologist should consist
in the choice of the nuance that best agrees with the writing's
general level and the other, surrounding signs.

GRAPHOLOGICAL DICTIONARY

Aspects of the writing	Interpretation

1. ACCELERATED
Between *poised* and *rapid* (about 150 words per minute). See the table of signs of speed, p.281.

Quick reactions, activity

Je lis très peu, je vis au soleil

2. ADDRESS

To be interpreted according to the *Symbolism of Space*.

3. AERATED
Good distribution of the white spaces between the words and lines.

See Thinking and Intuition Types. Intelligence, mental clarity, objectivity. *If the writing is large and expanded* : generosity.

[handwriting sample]

4. AMENDED

Self-observation, exaggerated desire to do well. Mania about scruples.

[handwriting sample]

5. ANGULAR
Accentuation of the normal angles of the copybook, or replacement of the normal curves by angles, hard and brittle movements.

See strong libido. Predominant will, firmness, tenacity, intransigence, obstinacy, contrary and stubborn spirit, anger (especially with firm pressure). The writing of the combative type. Inadaptability, lack of flexibility, lack of understanding. Gruff character, a nature that is virile to the detriment of the emotive and sensitive side (Anima).

[handwriting sample]

6. ANIMATED
Amplification of the strokes, agility and mobility of the writing trail.

See strong libido, in progression. Extraversion. Feeling Type.
Activity, imagination, vivacity, euphoria, easy contact with others, communicative nature.

7. ARCADIC
Exaggeration of the normal curves and connections in the form of an arc.

See Introversion.
(a) Often a showy writing; distant pride, arrogance, a *withdrawn character*, discretion, secretiveness, complicated character, coldness, egoism. Dissimulation. The preceding is valid for *writing that is arcadic in its letter forms (m, n, u)*.
(b) *Arcades in a superior writing*: evident sometimes only in connections and combinations, are, more a sign of an intense inner life, of creative imagination, of artistic talent, constructive leanings.

8. ARCADIC, semi-angular

A closed character, cold, conventional.

9. ARTIFICIAL
Affected, disguised, systematic,
together with empty and
pretentious forms.

Tensing, often a hidden and over-
compensated inferiority complex.
Hysteria.
Fashionable forms :
worldly pride and snobbery.
Original forms : a seeking for
originality, desire to be different,
egocentricity, lack of taste and
naturalness, pretention, dissimulation. Fear. Aesthetically unsuccessful artificial writing is found
among artists, painters and
designers. See introverted Sensation Type.

ravitaillement général

10. AUTOMATIC
Stereotyped movements tending to
monotony; mechanical writing.

See libido, blocked or in regression.
Introversion, with a tendency to
obsession. Complexes. Repression. Lack of personality, lack of
flexibility and adaptability, of sensitivity and imagination. Manias.
Inner emptiness.
Automatic writing is found among
certain lunatics, where it becomes
stereotyped, empty of expression.

être considérée comme délirée
observations des divers aviateurs

11. BLURRED
With poorly defined confined contours, slurred.

See libido, weak or in regression.
General slackness.
Mediocre precision and energy.
Inconstant character.
With thready writing : sign of fatigue, depression that is fleeting, overwork. Sign of instability.

Veuillz agreer, Monsieur, l'assurance de mes sentiments les meilleurs

12. BROKEN
Frequent breaks in the stroke.

See libido, weak or in regression.
Pathological condition (respiratory and cardiac). Impeded activity.
Broken lower extensions in female writings : sometimes appear after operations.

vœux pour la nouvelle année

13(a). CENTRIFUGAL
Movement of the finals and free strokes directed upward, to the right.

(a) See Extraversion.
Independence. Vivacity, aggressiveness, rebellious spirit. High aspirations.

Veuillez, je vous

234

13(b). CENTRIFUGAL

(b) *At the beginning of words* : systematic objection, rancour in debate.

[handwritten: bienveillante]

14. CENTRIPETAL
Final strokes amplified and complicated by a stroke directed leftward.

Egoism. Calculated reserve that leads to falsehood (Crépieux-Jamin). It is often found with other signs of insincerity.

[handwritten: Mademoiselle]

15. CLEAR
With fine organisation, very legible and free of any complications.

Mental clarity, sound judgement, simplicity, sincerity, good sense (see *Aerated*).

16. CLUBBED

See *Inhibited* writing.

[handwritten signatures]

17. WITH SMALL COILS Good-natured underhandedness
and insincerity.

18. COMBINED

Superior degree of organisation, by virtue of quick, original combinations.

See libido in progression, Thinking, Intuition Types. Sure sign of intelligence and general culture (Crépieux-Jamin). Synthetic and independent thinking. Rhythmic, ventilated and combined writing : superior Formlevel (Klages).

19. COMPACT Contraction. Concentration.
Opposite of aerated writing. Reality sense. Heaviness.

20. COMPLICATED
Useless strokes in the formation of the letters.

Finicky, meticulous natures. Lack of openness and simplicity. Coquetry (Crépieux-Jamin).

21. CONCAVE
Lines sunken in the middle.

Discouragement followed by effort to be free of it. Uneasiness. Reflection of a poor physical condition. Sign of instability.

22. CONNECTED
Entire words or groups of 5 or 6 letters written at a stroke.

See libido in progression, Thinking Type.
Continuity in though or effort.
In a superior general level : logic, memory, intelligence.

23. OVER-CONNECTED
Letters and words connected without interruption. See example 8 in the Dictionary.

Obstinacy in ideas, closed to the arguments of others, obsessive ideas. Excess of logic, sophistry.
With large garlands : it belongs with Dr. Kretschmer's cyclothymic type. *With right-slanted, firmly pressured writing* : fanaticism.

24. CONVENTIONAL
(Sacré-Coeur)

Conformity. "Persona" writing.

25. CONVEX
Lines arched in the middle.

Initial effort that is not sustained.
Fight against depression. Sign of
instability.

26. COPYBOOK
Painstaking, regular writing.

See blocked libido.
Without personality. "Good pupil".
Copybook writing often hides full-
blown repressions and neuroses of
all kinds.

27. DESCENDING
Lines decline from left to right.

See libido, weak or in regression. Depression, fatigue, discouragement, pessimism, melancholy, passive neurosis. Setback or presentiment of decline.

28. DIMINISHING
Words diminishing in height, forming a triangle.

See weak libido.
Finesse, cunning, falsity, dissimulation. Aptitude for probing others without allowing oneself to be fathomed (Michon).
Crépieux-Jamin opposes this interpretation and insists on the meanings of sensitivity, fatigue, exhaustion, unsustained effort.
These two interpretations can be reconciled, in that the features discovered by Michon derive naturally from those pointed out by Crépieux-Jamin : the weak use of the weapons within their power : finesse among superior people; dissimulation among inferior people.

29. DISCORDANT
Badly balanced, disparate in size, form, etc.

Sure sign of neurosis :
imbalance, inner tension, unresolved conflicts between tendencies coming from the conscious and the unconscious. Indecision, changing mood, caprice, lack of objectivity, *ambivalence*. Unco-ordinated action, ineffective action, Discordant writing is peculiar to those who unconsciously sabotage their lives. Sign of instability and confusion.

30. DISORGANISED

In which the graphic structures, formerly organised, have been altered by age, illness or intoxication. (see *shaky* writing).

If the general harmony of the writing persists, one must consider that the disorganisation is partial, and must evaluate the qualities that exist.

31. DOUBLE-JOINED

Ovals are double-looped by means of a left-tending movement.

See libido in regression, exaggerated Introversion, flight complex. Egocentricity, closed-in character, distrust, dissimulation, falsity.

240

32. DYNAMIC
Rapid, powerful, progressive, expanded, ascending.

See strong libido, in progression, Extraversion.
Strong vitality. Psychic energy that is freely discharged. Vibrant activity, euphoria, love of life, good health. Nervous. Bilious (Dr. Carton).
Rapid thinking. Impatience. Conviction. Communicates his enthusiasm to others.

33. EFFERVESCENT
Very uneven in size, in direction, thin, jerky.

Intensity of life.
Nervous temperament, explosive. Inconstancy, excessive sensitivity, impatience, enterprising spirit that is not maintained, erratic volitional power.

34. EMBELLISHED
Ornamented with flourishes or useless strokes.

See Extraversion, Sensation Type. Over-compensation for an inferiority complex.
Ostentation, bad taste flaunted, boasting, fatuity, pretentiousness, overflowing egocentric imagination. The writer delights in superfluous details.

35. ENLARGING
Words increase in size.

See Extraversion.
Opening-up of the soul, frankness, spontaneity. Penchant for speaking out, to the point of becoming offensive. Characteristic of childish writing. Persists among adults who retain the candid fervour of children. (Creative artists).

36. ENRICHED

See embellished writing.

37. EXPANDED
General amplification of all movements in a progressive direction.

See libido in progression, Extraversion, Feeling Type.
Communicative nature, openness, imprudence, generosity, waste, dissipation, garrulity, state of euphoria.
With original forms : artistic talents, need to exteriorise, to create.

38. FALSE CONNECTIONS

Difficulty in co-ordination of movements. Fatigue. Nervousness.

39. FALTERING
Fragile, unsteady, discordant in direction.

Weak libido.
Soft character, easily influenced. Fatigue, asthenia.

40. FILIFORM - (THREADY)
Like an unravelled thread.
The inner letters replaced by a generally undulating stroke.

General cause : desire for simplification which, in active people, procures : economy of time and movement; in sick people : economy of effort; in false and fugitive natures : the vagueness they seek (Crépieux-Jamin).
When there is disproportion between capitals and small letters : a classic sign of the inferiority complex with over-compensation. See weak libido.
Sign of instability. Predisposition to neuroses. Fertile ground for complexes.
Slight resistance to the blows in life. Diplomacy, avoidance of decisions and responsibilities. Flexibility. A character that is protean, depending on the surroundings. Protective colouration. *In a superior writing, with combinations* : inventive mind (see Intuition Type). *With descending lines* : fatigue, serious depressions, exhaustion.

41. FINALS : WITH CENTRIPETAL FINALS	Monopolising.

1, rue Legendre

42. FINALS : WITH OPEN-CURVE FINALS	See Extraversion. Feeling Type. Amiability, gracious manners.

Fontaine

43. FINALS : WITH PROLONGED FINALS Downward, in a movement of nervous relaxation.	Nervousness, irritability, nervous discharge.

l'expression de ma considération

44. FINALS : WITH SHORT FINALS	See Introversion. Discretion, reserve.

Mardi

45. FINE A writing trail that is fine and more or less thin.	See Introversion, Thinking, Intuition Types. Delicate health, *sensitivity*, deli- cacy, tact, timidity, lack of practical sense, cerebral activity. This writing, especially when it is venti- lated and connected, progressive and combined, is found among scientists. ***With prolonged upper*** ***extensions*** : mystical feeling.

46. FIRM

Strongly *pressured* writing trail, in relief, precise and resolute.

See strong libido, in progression. Virile character (see *Animus*). Preponderance of will. Good vital balance. Energetic character, an achiever. Composure. Leadership ability. *With angular writing* : firmness to the point of intransigence, obstinacy, impermeability to outside influences, brutality. *With large, angular writing* : courage and assurance. Sign of stability, the writing of a man of action.

Librairie Stock

47. FORWARD-THRUSTING (THROWN)

Graphic structures that are thrown forward as extensions, in a burst of speed.

See libido in progression, Extraversion.
Impulsiveness, spontaneity, impatience, over-activity, excitement, agitation, violence, combative nature, passionate outbursts. Zeal flaring up that is as quickly extinguished.
Forward-thrusting strokes that cover the word : spirit of domination. Feeling of superiority, especially in a large, artificial writing with pronounced capital letters.
Firm, forward-thrusting writing : will power.

Conrad

FOXTAILS

See *Margins, Plunging lines.*

48. FULL
Loops enlarged without being inflated.

See Thinking and Intuition Types. Intelligence, mental clarity, objectivity. *If the writing is large and expanded* : generosity.

Marces Srueore de greie

49. GARLANDED
Letters "n", "m", "u".

See Extraversion, Feeling type. Small garland : Thinking Type, Introversion. Receptivity, affection, gentleness; flexibility, adaptability, easily influenced. Devotion. *With small, combined writing* : sign of fast, flexible thinking. Found among many scientists.
Soft, light, monotonous garlands : melancholy.
"Ringed" garlands : often found among writers.
Large, right-slanted and expanded writing : characterises Dr. Kretschmer's cyclothymic type. Activity, contact with others. Easy exteriorisation.

ravie comme un enfant

50. GROUPED

In which the letters are neither wholly connected nor separated from each other, but connected in little groups, variable in number.

See libido in progression, Thinking and Intuition Types.
This sign is related to the writer's faculty for intellectual adaptation. Flexibility, cleverness, the art of intelligent achievement; it is the mark of aptitude for varying activity (Crépieux-Jamin, *ABC de la graphologie*).

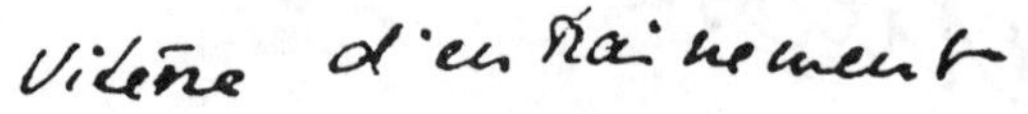

Vitêne d'en Raineument

51. HARMONIOUS

Clear and well-proportioned. (see Louis Jouvet's combined writing, p.265)

Harmony of functions and tendencies.
See libido in progression.

[handwritten manuscript text]

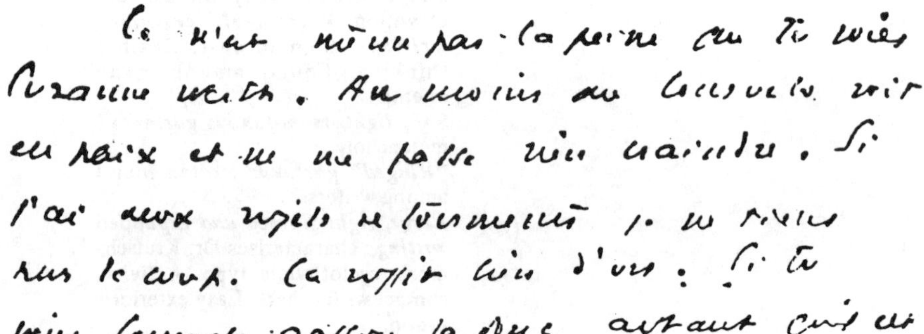

52. HEAVY (thick)

Brings together the characteristics of firm writing and pastose writing.

See strong libido, Sensation Type.
With inferior level : sensuality, preponderance of instinctive and vegetative life. The writing of

HEAVY, continued

heavy eaters and great drinkers. Materialism. Physical strength. Congestive condition. Brutal and unscrupulous opportunism. Authoritarianism. Scepticism. Practical sense and muscular activity. Often, lack of sensitivity, tact and delicacy.
With superior level : is often found among artists.

PARIS

53. HOMOGENEOUS

Crépieux-Jamin defines *homogeneous* writing as :
"the unification of the movements into a personal style without taking account of the value of the qualities .... . It is a sign of good equilibrium and constancy". It therefore supports the same characteristics in a writing without descending into the monotony created by absolute regularity.

Ayant pris connaissance de l'annonce qui a été insérée dans ", du 5 décembre, j'ai l'honneur de vous faire

54. HOOKS -
WITH SMALL HOOKS

Egoism, monopolising.

si l'honneur

55. INFLATED
Exaggeration of the ovals and
loops as a result of expansion.

See exaggerated Extraversion,
over-compensation of complexes.
Hysteria.
Inflation of the empirical Ego,
pride, *if the capital letters are
exaggerated*, excited sensuality
(*lower extensions*), lack of
discrimination, lying, mythomania,
flight into unreality. Ostentatious
spending, especially *with large
writing.*

Bourgogne

56. INHARMONIOUS

See *Discordant* writing.

*Je viens vous remercier de la
avec laquelle vous vous occupez de m
que ce docteur réussira et saurer
soma qui est actuellement dans un état*

57(a) and (b). INHIBITED

Shares common ground with writings that are hesitant, unfinished, punctuated, slowed down, left-slanted, amended, clubbed, suspended, etc.
Stops in the scriptural rhythm.

See libido, blocked or in regression. Inferiority complex. Difficulties with the self-esteem function.
Inhibited writing reflects the whole gamut of neurotic symptoms that arrest the free development of energy and lead to psychic and physical disturbances.
General nervousness, irritability, repression, pauses and disturbances in the free development of the personal rhythm, inner conflicts (*especially with irregular writing*).
Morbid self-observation, susceptibility, anxious desire to do well, hairsplitting mind (*amended writing*).
Weakness, lack of character, whence the interpretation of falsity (*suspended writing*).
Hesitation, doubt, lack of self-confidence, distrust (*hesitant, slowed-down, punctuated writings*).
Protest against authority (*left-slanted writing*).
Brutal discharge of energy repressed for too long. Crises, scenes, (*clubbed writing*).
Obsessive ideas (*in mechanical writing, rigid, too connected and regular*).
Briefly : inhibitions of all kinds, depression, timidity, awkwardness, trouble attracting success, fear of the other sex, inadaptability. Sign of instability and confusion.

INHIBITED, continued

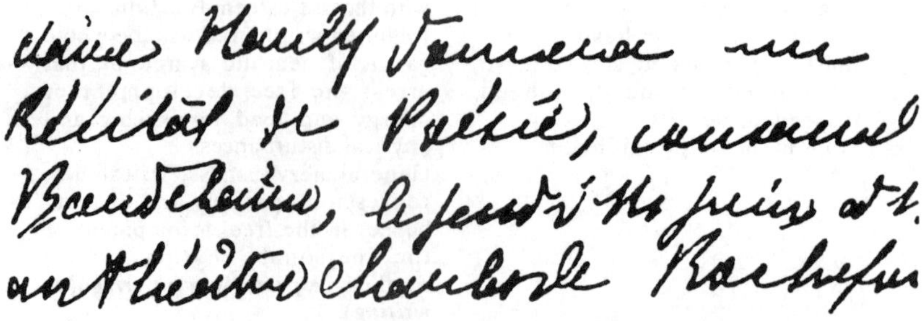

[handwritten text]

58. IRREGULAR

Writing irregular in all categories, without attaining discordancy.

A certain sign of sensitivity and emotivity. The smaller and more repeated the irregularities, the stronger are the corresponding emotions. (Crépieux-Jamin, *ABC*). *Irregular and rhythmic* : see Intuition Type. Preponderance of affective tendencies over reason and will, weak or unleashed libido according to the general aspect of the writing, Impulsiveness, little resistance to outside influences. Often found in neurotics. Instability, changing mood, caprice, fantasy. *In a superior writing* : flexible mind; *with expanded loops* : imagination. *With angular writing* : characteristic of the schizothymic type as defined by Dr. Kretschmer. Irregularity does not exclude rhythm. *Slightly irregular and rhythmic writing*: impressionability of a deep person. *Very irregular and rhythmic* : excessive impressionability renders life painful.

[handwritten text]

59. JERKY
Synonym : agitated;
Antonym : calm.

Disposition to neuroses. The emotions or fatigue, among the nervous types, produce vaso-motor disturbances, agitation, quiverings, palpitations, which have an impact on the writing through sudden irregularities of form, direction and especially, of size.

Jerky writing, through its continuous contrasts, is an indisputable sign of hypersensitivity (Crépieux-Jamin).

Irritation, impulsiveness, anger, imbalance.

With wide spacing : isolation, lack of contact with others, With sharp-pointed strokes : aggressiveness, bitterness.

In a thready writing:inconsistency.
In an angular writing : the egoism typical of neurotics.

It is the writing of the greatly nervous type.

60(a). JUXTAPOSED
(DISCONNECTED)
Letters of the words separated from each other.

See Intuition Type.

For Abbé Michon, the sign of intuition. Crépieux-Jamin categorically rejects that interpretation, emphasising that juxtaposed writing, by its discontinuity, always indicates inhibition. For him, it is a sign of slowed up activity and debility. He points out that it is not combined.

I consider it a sign of debility *in a weak writing*, a sign of illogicality in an *inferior* writing. *In a superior writing* it expresses irrational associative and intuitive ideas.

JUXTAPOSED, continued

It may include a few combined strokes and thus characterise intuitive thinking.

rubrique théâtrale reparait Samedi, de passer cette Sauvage et de report

60(b). JUXTAPOSED AND COMBINED

Intuition. Original ideas.

61. LARGE
Small letter heights of 2 1/2 mm to 4mm.

See libido, strong or in progression. Extraversion, Feeling and Sensation Types.
Self-esteem, pride, vanity, euphoria, enthusiasm, activity. *With combined writing* : imagination, intuition.

62. VERY LARGE

Larger than the above dimensions.

See Extraversion.
Displacement of energy onto the surface, the need to amaze one's circle of friends, elevation of self-esteem, showing off. The writing of film-stars.

With exaggerated capitals : Hysteria. Morbid inflation of the Ego. Mythomania. Ostentatious spending. The need to feign value in order to compensate for feelings of inferiority.

63. LASSOS

Horizontal forward-thrown stroke coming back over itself. Most often the stroke is bent to the left.

For Abbé Michon, who had noticed it especially in female writings : coquetry, desire to be noticed, to create an effect, to be loved, to attract others to oneself, skill at setting a snare. *If the lasso is very complicated* : we have a schemer. Crépieux-Jamin adds, *with repeated lassos* : ambitious intrigues, a willingness to hatch plots and intrigues to satisfy passions.

One can also add, *in the paraph* : business cleverness.

64. LEFTWARD SLANT
Leftward slant of the letters surpasses 90 degrees.

See libido in regression. Repression, fear, timidity, coldness, tendency to negativism; in the young, to rebellion. Distrust, dissimulation. Pride. The writer surrounds himself with mystery.
Left-slanted writing is a form of defence that often hides a feeling of inferiority.

65. LIGHT
Slightly pressured writings.

Thinking, Intuition Types. Delicacy, congenital fragility, sensitivity; *with weak lower extensions* : lack of reality sense. Impressionability, spiritual qualities; *if very irregular* : slight character; *if spread out and rapid* : superficiality. *If thready* : inconsistent, elusive character. In a good level writing : elegance of mind. *Writing that is light, progressive, combined, simplified* : the writing of scientists with creative minds.

66. LIMPID
Limpidity is the mark of the greatest clarity. Sharpness of

See Thinking, Intuition Types. *In a writing of superior level* : mental clarity, simplicity, sincerity, ingenuousness.

LIMPID, continued
stroke, legibility, harmonious
organisation.

Je suis limpiet

67. LOW
Foreshortened upper and lower extensions.

See libido, weak or in regression. *In a superior writing* : renunciation of active and sexual life to the benefit of the inner life. Introversion. *In a conventional and enlarged writing* : predominance of the empirical ego, egocentricity.

*En vous en remerciant
à l'avance, je vous prie de*

68. LOWER EXTENSIONS -
WITH TRIANGULAR LOWER
EXTENSIONS

See Extraversion. Hysteria.
Vanity, spirit of domination.

Jeanne Gille

69. LYRICAL "d"   Poetic inspiration. Imagination. Meditation.

comprend un sentiment (d'ailleurs lé et un grand désir de considérat

70. MARGINS   See table, page 280

Left Margins

Regular	Order, self-confidence, will power.
Irregular	Fantasy, lack of order and discipline.
Widening	Impulsiveness, generosity, extraversion.
Wide	Generosity, spontaneity, extraversion.
Very wide	Carelessness, prodigality.
Narrowing	Prudence, distrust, introversion. The writer catches himself again after having made a spontaneous movement.
No Margin	Economical character, prudent. Introversion.
Typographic	*With other signs that confirm this indication* : avarice, fear, distrust, self-doubt. Taste, culture.

Right Margin

Wide	Carelessness, confidence.
Plunging lines (foxtails) (piled-up words descending at the end of lines).	Poor organisation as to time and money. Lack of foresight.

71. MONOTONOUS
Uniform, lifeless.

See libido, weak, or in regression. Lack of personality, apathy, indolence, slackness, boredome, melancholy, discouragement, resignation.

la population ayant répondu avec empressement, la liste des

72. MUDDY
Thick, flooded structures, loops and ovals ink-filled.

See blocked libido, Sensation Type, anal complex. High blood pressure, congestive condition, sensuality, gluttony, disorder, amorality, lack of discrimination, exaggerated egoism, heavy spirit, lack of drive, depression, illness. Lack of tact and delicacy.

naturelle.

73. NARROW
Compressed loops, letters too close together.

See Introversion, inferiority and anal complex. Fear. Apprehension, contraction, repression timidity, inhibition, lack of self-confidence, distrust, embittered, avarice.

Avec tous nos remerciements

74. ORGANISED
Denotes a writing sufficiently evolved to be executed effortlessly and without awkwardness.

Allows a graphological interpretation.

Vieus de rejevoir en même temps q de mon ami Girard avec mes devoirs

75. PALE
Characteristics stifled to achieve an insipid correctness.
(*Editor's note:* No variation between up/down strokes, no intensity, even pressure in all directions.)

See libido, weak or in regression. Repression, lack of personality, self-effacement, modesty, timidity, sometimes hypocrisy. The faculties are asleep, frozen, unused (Crépieux-Jamin).
Tedious characters, "wet blankets". Conventional people, conformists.

croire, Monsieur le Docteur, à mes sentiments respectueux

76(a). PASTOSE
Heavy, soft and greasy, with not very precise borders.

See Sensation Type.
With rhythm and original forms : sensuality, plastic arts. The writer obeys his instinctive tendencies.
With a soft writing : negligence.

cotte besühl hätte. auch mal was für

76(b). PASTOSE

Ta par définition, je suis content d'avoir l'avenir nous remettra t'il de ci, de là sa

77. SLIGHTLY PASTOSE WITH A VELVETY STROKE

Love of life, artistic sense. See Feeling and Sensation Types.

Chère Madame,

78. PLUNGING (FOXTAILS)
(see table, p.280)

Accentuated degree of descending writing.

79. POISED
Care in execution of the writing (100 letters per minute, Crépieux-Jamin). See the table of the signs of speed, p.281.

See Introversion.
Will power, moderation, calmness, reflective mind, prudence, self-control.

voulez m'envoyer de nouveau l'emballeur ferai une nouvelle expédition, un peu plu

80. PRECIPITATE
See the table of the signs of speed, p.281.

See libido in progression, Extraversion, Intuition Type. Lively mind, great activity, imprudence, impatience, agitation. *If there are other signs of instability and lack of balance* : active neurosis.

81. PRECISE
Contours precise and without smudging.

Thinking, Intuition Types. Good vital balance, delicate but resistant. Moderate energy. Perseverance. *In a regular writing* : will power, self-confidence. Mind that is precise, organised, clear. Objectivity. *With angular writing* : dryness of heart. Puritanism. Sign of stability.

82. DISPLACED PRESSURE
Carried onto the upstrokes.

Forced libido;
lack of naturalness.

83. PROGRESSIVE -
    OR RIGHT-TENDING

See libido in progression. Thinking type, Extraversion.
Fast, co-ordinated reactions and thoughts. Intelligence, activity, general superiority, cultured mind.

84. PROLONGED
    DOWNWARDS

See Sensation Type.
Physical activity, practical interests. *With strong pressure and well developed loops* : predominant sexuality.

85. PROLONGED UP AND
    DOWN

See Extraversion : perpetual dissatisfaction, need for change, agitation, over-activity, absence of concentration, lack of balance.

86. PROLONGED UPWARDS

Intellectual and spiritual tendencies, idealistic aspirations.

262

87. RAPID
(More than 180 letters per minute, Crépieux-Jamin). See the table of the signs of speed, p.281.

See libido in progression.
Quick reactions, intellectual superiority, culture, activity.

Je vous demande de bien vouloir

88. REGRESSIVE -
or LEFT-TENDING
In which the strokes are in a direction opposite to the movement of the writing trail.

See libido, in regression or blocked.
Lack of spontaneity. Lack of adaptation, egoism, tendency to dissimulation, recoiled from life. Egocentricity, reflecting upon the self. Coquetry.
The writing of *extraverted* types often has regressive strokes, which indicate the unconscious *introverted tendencies* as opposed to the conscious attitude.

89. REGRESSIVE -
With strong regressive strokes

Monopolising

90(a). REGULAR

D'un sentiment inconnu

90(b). REGULAR

Constancy in the size and spacing of the letters. Moderate, organised writing.

(a) See strong libido, in progression. Preponderance of will power over the emotive and instinctive life. **With an angular, strongly pressured writing** : great vital energy, physical strength, goal-oriented will power.
(b) Sense of duty, preponderance of conscious tendencies over unconscious tendencies in the form of discipline.
But this preponderance of the conscious tendencies involves stifling of the unconscious tendencies and their riches and, consequently, an impoverishment. The person becomes mechanical and estranged from the deep springs of his being.
A sign of stability. Is often found in "Persona" writings.

*Je suis en congé dehors la première semaine
l'oct. et le repos absolu m'est encore imposé je
eux mois au moins. Je vais bp mieux déjà de.
suis que je suis ici : Le soleil est miraculeux –*

91. IN RELIEF

Contrast between the upstrokes and downstrokes, with precise edges.

See strong libido, in progression. Good vital balance, endurance, resistance to outside influences, a self-assertive personality.
A sign of stability and will power.

*le temps passe si vite qu'il
laisse pas le loisir de me rec*

264

92a. RHYTHMIC

Klages defines rhythm as a succession of movements that are harmonious and are repeated without ever entirely resembling each other. It is the natural movement of the sea, of the fall of the leaves. It is the very expression of life. Life ignores geometric and chronometric identity, mechanisation.

One can *measure* the regularity of the writing (which never reaches that of a machine), but one can only *feel* the rhythm.

Rhythmic writing is the most important element of Klages's Form Level.

One must be on one's guard against the confusion that could be created between the Klagesian concept of "Life" and vitality. A writing of high Form Level does not necessarily indicate a strong vitality, or the degree of affectivity, which is, indicated more by the irregularity.

See strong libido in progression. Depth and intensity of the personality. Spontaneity. Sincerity. Harmony of tendencies and functions.

èle - Je regrette que vous ne soyez pas
ici . ne sur avant de l'écrire -
"papier" ne servira ni Jean Giraudoux
ni : et cela ne fait : ici que ce
ne fatigue bonne soi "honnête"
que je vous aime bien

Louis Jouvet

...es also, forgive the fact
this letter comes so late,
really been unable to cope
with my business in the way
I should.

Laurence Olivier

Ex. 92(b) (Louis Jouvet) and 92(c) (Laurence Olivier).

Rhythmic and combined writings. Superior general level.

93. RIGHT-SLANTED
Slanted to the right, forming an angle of less than 45 degrees with the horizontal line.

See Extraversion, Feeling, Sensation Type.

Activity, ardour.

In a light writing : impressionability, proneness to influence, subjectivity. Affective tendencies take primacy over reason.

With signs of enthusiasm, firm or pastose pressure : passion.

94. RIGHT-TENDING

See *progressive* writing.

95. RIGID
Inflexibility in all directions.

Repression, trouble with displacement of the libido, complexes.

Lack of adaptation, disposition to obsessional neuroses. Inflexibility, precision, severity, hardness. Repeated small irregularities (in the size of the small letters) sometimes reveal, in a rigid writing, the sensibility and emotivity hidden behind the immutable facade, the characteristic play between the "Persona" and the unconscious tendencies.

A sign of stability.

Lack of social feeling, egoism.

96. RISING
Ascending lines.

See libido in progression, Extra-version.
Activity, ambition, optimism, self-confidence, passionate outburst.
Climbing : exaltation.

97. RISING AND DESCENDING

Sudden change of mood. Neurosis. Instability. Irritability.

98. ROUNDED
Replacement of angles by curves and accentuation of normal copybook curves.

See Feeling Type.
Adaptability, sociability ranging from affability to inconsistency.
If large and right-slanted : extra-version, tendency to numerous projections. *If nourished and right-slanted* : warm-heartedness.
If wide and right-slanted : ease and spontaneity of manner. *Small and rounded* : Thinking Type.

SACRÉ-COEUR   see *Conventional* writing.

99. SHAKY   See weak libido.
Jerky in the stroke.   Different causes : swaying of the
                                objects around us, cold, fatigue, *old
                                age*, fear, irritation, all the
                                emotions.   Certain poisonous
                                substances.

100. SHARP-POINTED   See Thinking Type.
Finals and t-bars often sharp- Irritability, aggressiveness, com-
pointed.   bativeness, impatience, vivacity,
                                caustic and critical spirit, spite-
                                fulness, bad temper, nervous
                                violence, vindictive spirit.

SIGNATURE :
See the end of the dictionary, p.282

101. SIMPLIFIED   See libido in progression, intro-
Reduction of the writing to its version, Thinking and Intuitive
simplest expression.   Types.

SIMPLIFIED, continued	Superior intelligence, culture, activity. The writer aims at the essential.

Si ino ay un lun de longs lomr liné , j'

102. SLACK
Soft, creeping writing, without relief, without tension, of uncertain direction.

See libido, weak or in regression. Physical and psychic deficiency, indifference, fatigue, softness, laziness, indecision, waste, general decadence. Sign of instability and discouragement.

Maman

103. SLOW
(Less than 100 letters per minute, Crépieux-Jamin). See the table of the signs of speed, p.281.

See libido blocked or in regression. Slow reactions. Slow, heavy mind. Mediocrity. Inactivity, hesitation, ignorance.

Tout d' abord je m' excuse

104. SMALL
The inner letters are less than 11/2 mm to 2mm in height.

See Introversion, Thinking Type.
With a good level : concentration, attention. Industry, withdrawal into self.
Modesty, finesse, cunning. Lack of self-confidence, inferiority complex, fear, meanness, susceptibility. See libido in regression.

SMALL, continued

Small, monotonous, garlanded : melancholy.
In a woman, *small* writing shows a preponderance of her masculine side (see Animus), cerebral activity, intellectual discipline (*with a superior level*).
Small, regular writing : finicky mind.
Small and complicated : see introverted Sensation Type.

avec le séjour chez ma Chère Tanti

105. SOARING
Thrust upward with a fast, light movement.

See libido in progression.
Feeling for the ideal, mystical impulse. *In a not very developed writing* : lack of discrimination. Practical joking.

Mon t- Valérien

106. SOBER
Sober, contained movements.

See Introversion, Thinking Type.
Moderation, reflection, modesty, good sense, order, system.
With angular writing : coldness of heart.

SOBER, continued

Dans cette période de décadence complète, on se tourne avec instinct ceux qui incarnent encore les qu... de notre race, et on se souvient a...

107. SPACED-OUT

Spacing between words exceeds that of one letter as indicated by the copybook.
Large spaces between lines.

See Introversion, Thinking Type. Isolation, distance, difficult social contact. Critical sense, objectivity to the detriment of spontaneous affectivity. Independence of character. *With a squeezed, vertical writing* : coldness, fear of life. *With a superior writing* : mental clarity, order, moderation, judgement.

Vous saverez non Curriculum vitae.

108. SPASMODIC

Sudden thickenings in a not very strongly pressured writing (spindles, dots, swellings).

Unconscious reflexes, preponderant instinctive and impulsive life. Sensual spasms and nervous contractions. Eroticism that is perverted, found often among inverts and vicious persons. Sexual repression that explodes into quarrels, over-activity, exaggerated avidity, or takes the form of gluttony (*swollen or spindle-shaped writing*). Excitement. Hysteria.
In filiform writing with large capitals : very marked inferiority complex with overcompensation.
A sign of instability and neurosis.

Recevez Monsieur mes très sincères

109. SPINDLE-SHAPED See *Spasmodic* writing.

Boulevard

110. SPREAD-OUT
Extreme degree of expanded writing. Letters widened at their base.

See exaggerated Extraversion. Feeling Type.
Vanity, nonchalance, carelessness, laziness, exuberance, dissipation. It is the writing of intrusive persons.

caractère

111. SQUEEZED
Letters and words very close together.

See Introversion, libido in regression.
Inhibition. Reserve, economy, lack of self-confidence, distrust, egoism, avarice, meanness, attention, order, circumspection.

cause aucunes des qualités, la connaissance de mon métier,

112. SUPERELEVATED
Superelevated writing is that which increases the height of certain letters with the help of elevations or prolongations.

See inferiority complex with its over-compensation in immoderate pride. Pretension of the weak. In apparently balanced writings it is sometimes the only sign of imbalance and of disturbances of the self-esteem.

SUPERELEVATED, continued

113. SUSPENDED

In which some writings are interrupted before their normal completion. (see *Inhibited* writing).

See weak libido.
A sign of inhibition. Fatigue. Many graphologists see in this a sign of insincerity. The occasional lie is often the result of weakness.
A sign of instability.

114. SWORDS

See spasmodic writing.
Violence, aggressiveness, angry outburst, excitement, exaggerated sensuality.

115. TANGLING LINES
In which the upper and lower extensions intermingle as a result of their excessive length.

Emotional tendencies dominate reason. Lack of clarity of mind. Agitation.
In round and inflated writing, blindness through an excess of sentimentality and of self-pride. Unnecessary complications.

116. THIN
Elongated, light, often narrow, dry general appearance.

See Introversion.
Preponderance of reason. Logical thinking takes primacy over imagination. Dryness. *In a right-slanted, rigid writing* : fanaticism.

THREADY

See *filiform*

THROWN

See *forward-thrusting*

117(a). TILES, ASCENDING
Words that rise and fall successively, always starting from the baseline.

See libido, weak or in regression.
Ascending tiles represent a constantly renewed effort, but without vigour.

117(b). TILES, DESCENDING
Words that rise and fall successively, always starting from the
baseline.

Descending tiles express obstinacy,
although without hope, the dull
stubbornness of an energy devoid
of drive (Crépieux-Jamin).
Belongs with many neuroses and is
often found with other signs of
instability in a writing.

118. TWISTED
Straight strokes become sinuous
and the bend of the curves is
sometimes exag-gerated to the
point of deformity.

See weak libido, blocked or in
regression.
Circulatory and endocrine disturbances, transitional physiological
periods, fatigue, frequent in the
period of puberty. I have observed
twisted strokes in women's
writings, especially after operations. Overwork. Twisted writing is
sometimes found with spasmodic
writing and indicates serious
physiological disturbances.
A sign of instability.

119. UNDERLINED
and other means of attracting attention :
change of slant of the letters, enlarging of certain words, etc.

In a clear, normal writing : need, for good reasons, to state precisely. *Excessive underlining* : pedantry, exaggeration, vehemence. Psychopathic tendencies. *Illogical underlinings* : absurdity, foolishness, mania.

120. UNDULATING WORDS
Characterised by the undulation of the strokes and lines.

A sign of instability.
Emotivity, uneasiness, inconsistency, weakness, exhaustion, hesitation, diplomacy, dissimulation. Great flexibility (*with signs of intelligence*). Is often found with other signs of insincerity (*coils*) and confirms the diagnosis of a spineless character.

121. UNFINISHED
Uncompleted structures.

See libido, weak or in regression. Sign of instability. *In a rapid writing* : means of simplification. Nonchalance, fatigue. *In a slow writing* : inhibition, debility, fatigue, exhaustion, indifference, lack of life and of interest, laziness, negligence.

122. UNNECESSARY LINES
Showing superfluous horizontal strokes over stems and below lower extensions.

Found among "hotheads", bad-tempered, but not bad people. Tendency to abrupt decisions.

123. UNORGANISED
Unevolved writing which shows lack of graphic culture.

The writing of children and illiterates. This writing does not allow a complete graphological analysis.

124. UNSTABLE

The characteristics vary from one specimen to another, or in the body of the same specimen.

See weak libido.

Disposition to complexes and neuroses. The instability of the writing reveals the mobility and fragility of attention and feelings. Unstable people are pleasure-seeking, versatile, weather vanes; their variability and weakness take them naturally toward lying and infidelity (Crépieux-Jamin).

VELVETY

See *pastose* writing.

125. VERTICAL

Perpendicular to the horizontal line.

Stability, firmness, reserve, coldness, composure, lack of spontaneity. Reason takes primacy over the heart. Pride. Distrust, egoism. *With firm writing* : sign of will power.

126. WEAK
Accentuated curves, slow, anaemic writing trail, without assurance.

See libido, weak or in regression.
Lack of energy, apathy, inactivity, heavy spirit; indolence, lack of initiative and interest. Lack of foresight, confusion, laziness.
Sign of instability.

127. WELL-NOURISHED
Sufficiently pressured, well inked.

See strong libido, in progression.
Sensation, Feeling Types.
Good vital balance, sustained energy, capacity for work.
With animated writing : sign of fearlessness, ardour and vigour.

DISPOSITION OF LINES AND MARGINS

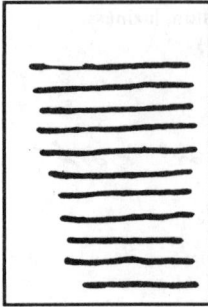

Widening margin   Typographical layout   Narrowing margin

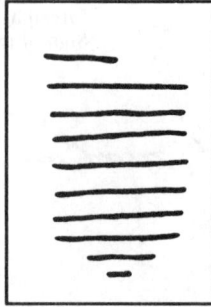

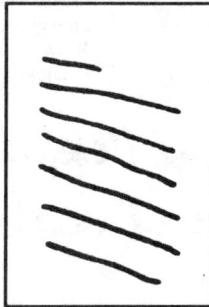

Rising lines   Falling lines   Plunging lines

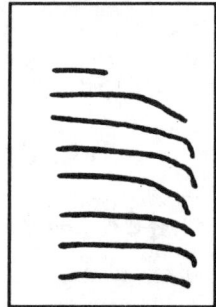

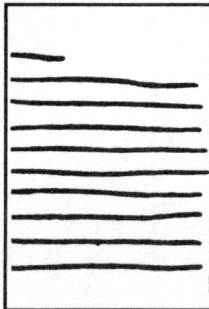

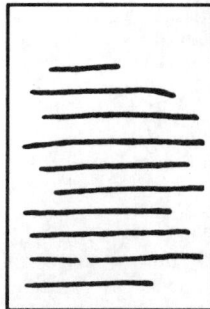

No margin   Irregular margin

PRINCIPAL SIGNS OF SPEED

Freedom of movement and rounded forms.
Progressive writing.
Simplified writing.
Dots and accents placed inexactly.
Joining of accents or t-bars to the following letter or word.
Last letters lessened in size.
Writing expanded at the end of lines.
Marked difference between downstrokes and upstrokes.
Left margin widening.
Rising lines.

PRINCIPAL SIGNS OF SLOWNESS

Regressive writing.
Shaky and broken forms.
Dots and accents carefully placed.
Interruption of the writing trail (broken, stippled writing).
Readjustments, amendments.
Writing carefully tended in its details.
Writing progressively increasing in size in the middle zone.
Pastose or soft writing.
All embellishments, adornments, scrolls, paraphs.

Robert Saudek placed the speed of the writing at the centre of his *Experiments With Handwriting.*

The list above is an extract from the tables he established.

If it is convenient to express the writing's degree of speed by the terms :
slow, poised, accelerated, fast, precipitate, we can say that :
In *slow* writing, the signs of slowness clearly predominate.
In *poised* writing, the signs of speed and slowness nearly balance each other.
Accelerated writing generally has several signs of speed.
In *rapid* writing, there is no longer any sign of slowness.
In *precipitate* writing, we find exaggerated signs of speed.

PUNCTUATION

Accents and dots placed high : Idealism, ambition, illusion.
Accents and dots ahead of the letters : Precipitation, enthusiasm, impetuosity.
Accents and dots placed exactly : Order, reflection.
Accents and dots placed low : Materialism, calculation, reflection.
Exclamation and Interrogation points in profusion : Exuberance. Extraversion pushed to excess.

THE SIGNATURE

We cannot interpret a signature in isolation, but study of the signature allows us to complete the interpretation of the text.

Signature larger than the text : Discordancy between what one is and what one wishes to appear; over-compensated inferiority complex.

Signature very far rightward : Libido in progression, extraversion.

Signature to the left : Libido in regression, distrust, introversion, lack of self-confidence.

Signature pushed very far leftward and reduced to initials : Libido in regression, exaggerated introversion, obsessive ideas and flight from life.

Large signature : Vitality, extraversion, exuberance, self-confidence, presumption.

Small signature : Introversion, modesty, simplicity.

Bô Yin Râ

C.G. Jung.

A. Einstein.

Simple signature without a paraph : Distinction. Introversion. Simplicity.
Preponderance of the inner life over the outer life. It is the signature of
thinkers.

Underlined signature : Will power, decision, firmness.

Signature with paraphs (see overleaf)

284

Signature with paraphs : Vanity, self-esteem, ambition, fantasy. Paraphs are a field in which the manifestations of the unconscious are given free reign.

Paraph surrounding the name : Dissimulation, desire to remain hidden.

Signature with large closed, entwined movements : Crafty mind, insincerity, dissimulation, cunning (Dr. Petiot).

Signature of Frobenious (explorer) : The violence of a man of action against whom nothing can resist. Extraversion, imagination, productiveness.

Signature of an engineer in which tools figure symbolically : Pincers, pliers.

286

Signature of a film director : This signature in the shape of a rainbow
makes one think of the scaffolds on which, between earth and sky, the
director turns in the course of "shooting" a film.

BIBLIOGRAPHY

PSYCHOLOGY

C. G. JUNG
- *Problèmes de l'Ame Moderne,* Preface by Dr. Roland Cahen, translated by Yves Le Lay, Buchet-Chastel, Corréa.
- *Types Psychologiques.* Preface and translation by Yves Le Lay. Georg, Geneva, Albin Michel.
- *Métamorphoses de l'Ame et ses Symboles.* Preface and translation by Yves Le Lay. Georg, Geneva, Albin Michel.
- *La Dialectique du Moi et de l'Inconscient.* Preface and adaptation by Dr. R. Cahen. Gallimard, 1961.
- *Psychologie et Alchimie.* Translation by Dr. R. Cahen and R. Picherot. Buchet-Chastel, Corréa, 1962.

Dr. FRANÇOISE ARETTE-DOLTO. *Psychoanalyse et Pédiatrie.* Amédée Legrand, edition, Paris 1940.

Dr. I. JACOBI. *La Psychologie de C.G. Jung.* Rascher, Zurich.

Dr. RENÉ ALLENDY. *L'Enfance Méconnue.* Mont-Blanc. Geneva.

Dr. OLIVER BRACHFELD. *Le Complexe d'Infériorité.* Mont-Blanc, Geneva.

ALFRED ADLER. *L'Enfant difficile.* Petite Bibliothèque. Payot.

Dr. KRETSCHMER. *Structure du Corps et Caractère.*

CHARLES BAUDOUIN.   - *L'Œuvre de C.G. Jung.*
                  - *Le Symbolisme du Rêve.* Stock.

ANIA TEILLARD.   - *Le Rêve, une Porte sur le Réel.* Stock.
                  - *La Dimension Inconnue.* La Baconnière.

A. MAEDER. *Vers la Guérison de l'Ame.* Delachaux et Niestlé.

GRAPHOLOGY

STRELETZKY. *L'Ecriture du Praticien.* Vigot, 1936.

G.E. MAGNAT.   - *Poésie de l'Ecriture.* Sack. Geneva.
               - *Suite à Poésie de l'Ecriture.* H. Sack. Geneva.

KLAGES.   - *Graphologie.* Stock.
               - *Expression du Caractère.* Delachaux.

SAUDEK. *Experiments with handwriting.* Allen Unwill, London.

PULVER. *Symbolisme de l'Ecriture.* Translated by Mard. Schmid and Maurice Delamain. Stock, 1953.

H. DE GOBINEAU. *Génétique de l'Ecriture.* Delachaux.

Dr. AJURIAGUERRA. *L'Ecriture de l'Enfant. La Rééducation de l'Ecriture.*

S. DELACHAUX. *La Graphologie de l'adaptation au travail.* Delachaux.

SAINT-MORAND-BRESARD. CHATINIERE-ROUGEMENT. PIERRE FOIX. *L'Orientation Professionnelle par la Graphologie.* Payot.

J. DUBOUCHET. *L'Analyse des Phénomènes Physiques et Psychiques et l'Ecriture.* Parthenon.

G. BEAUCHATAUD. *Apprenez la Graphologie.* Ed. J. Oliven.

R. TRILLAT. *Eléments de Graphologie Pratique. Précis de Graphologie.* Vigot.

ALSO PUBLISHED BY **SCRIPTOR BOOKS**

GRAPHOLOGY, VOL. I. The Interpretation of Handwriting,
by Renna Nezos, 315 pages, 70 handwriting samples.

ADVANCED GRAPHOLOGY, VOL. II. Twenty Lectures on Selected Subjects,
by Renna Nezos, 388 pages, 115 handwriting samples.

JUDICIAL GRAPHOLOGY, VOL. III.
by Renna Nezos, 178 pages, 13 illustrations.

LEARN GRAPHOLOGY. A practical course in fifteen lessons,
by Gabrielle Beauchataud, 320 pages, 217 handwriting samples.

CHARACTERS AND HANDWRITINGS,
by Emile Caille, 307 pages, 103 handwriting samples.

PSYCHOLOGY OF HANDWRITING,
by Dr. J.Ch. Gille-Maisani, 462 pages, 205 handwriting samples.

THE SOUL AND HANDWRITING,
by Ania Teillard, 288 pages, 210 handwriting samples.

THE SYMBOLISM OF HANDWRITING,
by Max Pulver, 371 pages, 186 handwriting samples.

GRAPHOLOGY AND THE ENNEAGRAM. Personality in Light and Shadow,
by Usha Mullan, 381 pages, 17 diagrams and 152 handwriting samples.

POETS' HANDWRITINGS,
by Dr. J.Ch. Gille-Maisani, 265 pages, 87 illustrations and handwriting
samples.

MANUAL OF GRAPHOLOGY,
by J. Peugeot, A. Lombard, M. de Noblens, 434 pages, 256 handwriting
samples.

All publications are available from *Scriptor Books*
123 Bickenhall Mansions, London W1H 3LB
Tel. 0171-935 9884, Fax 0171-935 6098, email: j.simopoulos@ic.ac.uk